Hearing Out
James T. Farrell

Hearing Out
James T. Farrell

Selected Lectures
edited by Donald Phelps

The Smith ✕ New York

Anne Heller, Text Editor
book design by Alfred P. Ingegno, Jr.
Copyright © 1985 by The Estate of James T. Farrell
First Edition/All Rights Reserved
Library of Congress Catalog Number: 84-52382
ISBN: 0-912292-75x
Printed at R.R Donnelley & Sons
Typography by ETC Graphics, NYC

Professor Edgar M. Branch of Miami University, Oxford, Ohio,
transcribed materials in these lectures.

contents

Introduction

James T. Farrell Having His Say

He was at once one of the most radically democratic of writers and one of the most jaggedly solitary. The curious, staid deliberation of his prose style, the spare, almost at times prim concreteness of the language, come not from that detachment which roosts on an eminence, but from the sense that he never failed to convey, of being in the thick of his neighbors' speech, thoughts, responses, fantasies, packets of history. Talk was his element in a way slightly different from almost any of his fellow American writers, because it was the flotsam-rich water in which he submerged himself; and, from the three-volume progress of Studs Lonigan's disintegration to the uncompleted *Universe of Time* saga, talk for him was the very conductor of actuality. His muse might have been a male one—spidery, Gabby Hayes-bearded Joe Gould, toting his perhaps-apocryphal Oral History of Mankind down Great Jones Street and up Waverly Place. Whether the History was, in fact, ever brought to some publishable dimensions, or ever completed, or ever begun, are secondary matters now; for a great and priestly American writer midwifed Gould's rough beast.

We do well to read, and reading, attempt to hear Farrell's lectures on literature, on democracy, on the illusions and realities of culture. I suspect many of his lectures (although I am still hardly more than excursion-tourist in that considerable territory) belong with his essays and short stories as crucial to his writing, a nurturing core; not "more important than" the best of his novels, but offering the most compactly rich perspective of his sensibility, thought and voice.

They require as much of the same kind of patience, in reading, as do some of his essays and much of the longer fiction. That phrase, "the same kind," requires a double underscore, however. One's patience with Farrell involves not a patronizing sigh, an elaborately relaxed posture, awaiting eight-year-old Jimmy's account of that day's history lesson. Our endurance of the longeurs, the gropings, the sometimes thick-though-strong-fingered locutions and cantilevered phrases, demands from us a recharged look at what we think we know about writing, about expression itself; the premiums we assign to novelty, filigreed articulateness, "brilliance." The considerations of style, of the artist's experience, of cultural influence and adornment that Farrell is constantly fingering may seem naive, backshelf, resolved or at least alloted their safe space, oh, decades ago. But then that patient, halting, discursive voice—with its rather startling, slightly mysterious aptitude

7

for placing such issues in relief—may beget in us still quieter, still firmer voices, asking: "But *were* they that easy? Hadn't you *better* look at them again?"

You may marvel, in reading and/or hearing him, how a man so generous of information, anecdote, the gait of his speech often approximating a purposeful saunter—how he could also keep his counsel so effectively. I am not referring, of course, to autobiographical diffidence, of which he had little or none, so far as Danny O'Neill books may suggest. I mean that he gives no shrift to the histrionics of your literary barnstormer, the packaging and burnishing skills involved in strutting one's profession and alleged vocation before an audience. There is a bone-lodged, absolute humility constantly defining words and bearing, which is initially next to appalling, ultimately bracing as only the deeply authentic can ever be. Many and many of his critics and reviewers have yet to get past that shock. He seems, himself, in the lectures and in the essays, of the realization that the vastness of actuality itself, of its history reborn and reincarnated in it each day (this latter became his guiding concern in *The Universe of Time*), can induce vertigo and possible collapse. He stands naked, with a hammer, an awl or chisel.

Every writer in one way or another redefines the specific. Farrell redefines it in terms of that offhand-seeming, deeply earnest colloquialism that we mark again and again in his lectures: a colloquialism that seems to find no lock on any door. His is one of the most austere of Irish voices; his humor is seldom whimsical—even when talking about his pontifical altertype, Mr. J.T. Fogarty—but, rather, sardonic, with the salt, bony irony of the non-vaudeville Irish. It is never a manner seeking to overpower and control: Although his self-esteem was robust enough, he eschewed just about every form of auctorial vanity. His colloquialism, rather, is a legitimate tone, seeking its own level and, as all such, creating that level among his truly attentive readers and auditors. (The question and answer sessions in this selection fully bear me out.) He is a superb crystallizer of the seemingly nebulous-abstract; he makes the utterances of a Mead, a Pierce or Whitehead seem, *be*, time after time, as graspable as a three-inch tabloid item; not through simplification but through a charged compression, a codifying intensity, which converts the quotes and summaries, legitimately, into a kind of news. His concision is that of a universal messenger bearing (although he scorned much journalistic fiction) the news. And again and again, some bright, impeccable salient—a quote from Alexander Herzen; one of Farrell's own observations on the use of imagery in fiction—will surface wonderfully from the opaque business of that colloquial style, smiting our attention like a poetic figure. I have been reminded, time after time in reviewing these lecture texts, how Farrell, whose actual verse often strikes me as weak and frostbitten, emerges as a poet, recurrently, in his prose.

I have found these lectures, in my own rereading—and the scant, reassembled memories of radio appearances and one speech to a Brooklyn College Young Socialists' Club—bracing and restorative; not only for the lean vitality that they impart to intellectual and cultural concerns, but for their collective reaffirmation of the writing act itself, through the reverent matter-of-factness with which Farrell addresses language and ideas and through his priestly rejection of dogmatic finalities. I have edited them largely for material which is repetitive of matter in companion essays (he never took notes); occasional superfluous stretches (although I have largely, properly I think, tried to preserve his roaming latitude of illustration and idea); and, in an instance or two, to clarify what was too-knottily uttered, or, simply, poorly transcribed from the tapes. The prose passages I have included were meant to serve a dual purpose: amplifying and confirming the lectures as ongoing conversations with an audience at large; and illustrating further Farrell's extraordinary, tough, loving faith in the ubiquity of ideas, and of immediate, fertile response to literature. I hope and pray that he may have been served half as well as, during his lifetime, he served us, his readers and fellow Americans.

Donald Phelps, New York City

Fear and Freedom

Speech delivered at Washington University,
St. Louis, Missouri, on March 3, 1954

One of the greatest voices for freedom, one of the men who felt and sensed what freedom meant, was Walt Whitman, a great American poet and a poet, I believe, of world stature. He wrote of freedom almost with a sense of ecstasy. Individualism *was* Walt Whitman—he was a poet of individuality. Individuality was something shared. There was a quality of empathy in his feeling for individuality. At one point he said that if he sees a wounded man, he feels his wounds. There wasn't the kind of aggressiveness or the kind of competitive sense of individuality that developed later in this country—there was none of that in Whitman.

I thought I would begin this lecture by reading from one of the last poems of *Leaves of Grass*—a poem entitled "So Long," which Whitman wrote when he was an old man.

> *To conclude, I announce what comes after me.*
> *I remember I said before my leaves sprang at all,*
> *I would raise my voice jocund and strong with reference to*
> *   consummations.*
>
> *When America does what was promis'd,*
> *When through these States walk a hundred millions of*
> *   superb persons,*
> *When the rest part away for superb persons and contribute to them,*
> *When breeds of the most perfect mothers denote America,*
> *Then to me and mine our due fruition.*
>
> *I have press'd through in my own right,*
> *I have sung the body and the soul, war and peace have I sung, and the*
> *   songs of life and death,*
> *And the songs of birth, and shown that there are many births.*
> *I have offer'd my style to every one, I have journey'd with confident*
> *   step;*
> *While my pleasure is yet at the full I whisper So long!*
> *And take the young woman's hand and the young man's hand for the*
> *   last time.*

I announce natural persons to arise,
I announce justice triumphant,
I announce uncompromising liberty and equality,
I announce the justification of candor and the justification
            of pride. . . .

I announce a life that shall be copious, vehement, spiritual, bold,
I announce an end that shall lightly and joyfully meet its translation.

I announce myriads of youths, beautiful, gigantic, sweet-blooded,
I announce a race of splendid and savage old men.

O thicker and faster—(So long!)
O crowding too close upon me,
I foresee too much, it means more than I thought,
It appears to me I am dying.

Now, we have possibly reached a situation in the world where we might be saying "So long" to freedom, to the dreams and the ideals that went into America. Abraham Lincoln, you know, described the United States as the last, best hope of the earth. Ideals of democracy are today threatened from within and from without. There is a kind of fear spreading; there is intimidation and there is self-intimidation. More and more people are being paralyzed, or else they are allowing themselves to feel this way. And unless we are able to resist the enemies of freedom, we are not likely ourselves to leave any kind of legacy such as that Walt Whitman left us; such as that of which Walt Whitman dreamed.

In the nineteenth century and the early part of the present one, it was believed that freedom was secure. It was believed that freedom was the norm and that tyranny was the exception, and that the crowned thrones and the tyrants of the world were tottering. In the twentieth century, after the end of the First World War, we have witnessed the rise of the most vicious, the most terrible and the most efficient tyrannies in the history of mankind, the rise of totalitarianism in Stalin's communist Russia, the Nazism of Hitler's Germany and fascism in Mussolini's Italy. Along with the rise of totalitarianism, many people have advanced the notion that people do not want freedom. The word "security" has been used again and again in emphasis of the claim that people will trade freedom for security.

From time to time there is a kind of a metaphysical argument that goes on about freedom. On the one hand we have democrats and liberals who developed a metaphysic of freedom based upon the idea of human perfectibility and upon metaphysical notions such as the idea of the general will. Counter to that is the idea, held by many conservative and reactionary thinkers, that man is incapable of freedom, that people must be guided and controlled. One of the great voices of reactionary thought was the late-eighteenth and early-nineteenth-century French thinker Joseph de Maistre, who held that man can create nothing; that man cannot create a free society but only God can; and that then it must be a society of authority. The arguments about freedom, when they are put in such a context, tend to mislead us and bring us back to the old argument about human nature: Is man good or bad? Was man born in original sin or was he not? Is he perfectable or is he evil?

We will not gain clarity if we think of freedom in these terms.

I would make the added point that, largely because of the spread and intensification of the influence of Freud and psychoanalysis generally, there has been an increasingly psychoanalytical approach to the question of freedom. There have been many indications that more and more people are attempting to interpret politics, as well as to discuss the question of freedom, in terms of psychology. Erich Fromm's book, with the excellent title *Escape from Freedom*, laid the basis for a conception held by some contemporary thinkers, one of them a German philosopher, Harkheimer, that there is such a thing as an authoritarian personality, and that the authoritarian personality is to be contrasted to the personality that resists control. There are two types, then—the type that wants authority and the type that does not want authority. The motive force of such a conception is largely psychological, largely Freudian.

In the same way, attempts have been made to explain complicated phenomena such as the rise of fascism and the rise of Joseph Stalin in terms of psychology. The American political scientist Frederick L. Schumann explains Stalin's victory over Leon Trotsky by stating that Lenin was Trotsky's father image, against which he was in revolt, and that in consequence he revolted against the same father image represented in Stalin; thus he was a son in revolt and he organized the plots of the Moscow trials; that Stalin was a good father image and Trotsky didn't want a good father image as authoritative as Stalin. This summary is partly parody, but it is the substance of one of Schumann's arguments which appears in a very serious and scholarly book, which is read in many colleges.

On the question of psychology and dictatorship, I would like to make just one point. I think it would be very easy to demonstrate that Hitler was a decidedly abnormal person. He was, in plain parlance, crazy. I think a good case could be made by psychologists to show that the late Joseph Stalin was a paranoid. But why is it, then, and under what conditions does an abnormal man become the leader of a great nation and play such a role in plunging the world into terror, misery and war? In the 1920's Hitler was the leader of a small, noisy, extremist group that was not taken very seriously. I recall that when I was a student in a comparative government class at the University of Chicago in 1925, in which my friend, Dr. Harold Lasswell, was my teacher, we were discussing various groups and factions in Germany and he mentioned the Nazis and the Ludendorf group and treated them as a lunatic fringe. I say this not to impute to Dr. Lasswell a lack of insight in advance; but I do wish to point out how we all make mistakes and how sometimes a small group or a small tendency may be fraught with great danger and may not be grasped by many; and yet the danger is deadly serious. I think one of the lessons of our time is that among the greatest political dangers mankind faces today is the danger of lunacy in politics. I think that Hitler and the Nazis most certainly demonstrate that.

Now, let's put this question to ourselves: Why was it that Hitler could not take power in 1923 or 1924? He did take power in 1932 and early 1933. Presumably, if we make a psychological explanation, he was sufficiently aberrant or abnormal in 1922, 1923 and 1924 to be diagnosed as possibly a psychotic, or to be called a nut, but social conditions, political conditions and attitudes in Germany at that time were such that he could not take power. Goebbels wrote: "No one knew how weak we were—how easily we could have been defeated at one time."

I make these remarks because I wish to emphasize the following point. The first sacrifice of freedom is in one's own mind; the first surrender is in one's heart. The beginning of the decline of liberty is with the rise of fear—fear of freedom and fear of one's fellow man.

At his ninetieth birthday celebration, the great American philosopher and liberal thinker, the great Dr. John Dewey, said in a very simple and moving speech that the greatest sin of all is to lose faith in your fellow man. It is by creating a pattern of fear, by destroying the confidence of people in themselves, by intimidation, that the process of the loss of liberty begins. There is a very illuminating story told about Napoleon at the time when he crowned himself Emperor of France. He was supposed to have asked an old soldier of the Army of Italy how he liked it. This old soldier, and I paraphrase him, said, "Sire, it was mighty fine, but it's too bad that ten thousand had to lose their heads so that this could not have happened." Now, I do not think that we can say there is in man a definite desire to be tyrannized, or that there is in man the opposite desire. There are both. We can state it in terms of love and hatred. Those who hate are afraid for people to be free. Those who have love in the sense that Walt Whitman had it welcome freedom.

I mentioned the current opinion that there is an authoritarian type of personality. I say that the authoritarian personality is not a special type; it's in all of us. There is a book by a French writer to be published in America in the fall; the writer's name is Suzanne Labin. The book will be called *Man Comes First*. It's an analysis of all the arguments against freedom and against democracy. It takes the abstract Marxist arguments, the Sartrist arguments, the Communist arguments and the fascist totalitarian arguments and answers every one of them. And Madame Labin also points out that there is a dormant fascist in all of us. There is a dormant totalitarianism in all of us. In other words, there is, at least, dormant fear in all of us.

Now, people are more or less afraid to be free in accordance with the price that must be paid. Where the price of freedom is too high, there are less people willing to take the risks of freedom. When the price of freedom is low, there are more people. The conscious, consistent, biding aim of dictators, totalitarians and would-be dictators is to create fear in a country. We can see an example of this in the Soviet Union and the stricken countries behind the Iron Curtain. We have there a sixth to a fifth of the world governed by millions of secret policemen. Any country, when there are millions of secret policemen at large in it, is a regime of fear. The purpose of secret policemen is to frighten people. Fear, the creation of fear, is the conscious aim of all those who would destroy freedom, as Hitler said, in effect, in *Mein Kampf*.

I think we ought to view fear of freedom and the capacity of man for freedom in these terms rather than in abstract metaphysical jargon, in which we counterpose general arguments against what we know of the nature of man and create a metaphysics of democracy and of reaction. If we do that we shall delude ourselves. And I think that if we overextend Freudian analysis at the present time, and treat the question of the capacity of man for freedom in terms of the individual psychology of various leaders, we shall do the same.

With that said, I would like to say that one realm in which we find efforts made to impose fear, and which is of great consequence, is the realm of culture. The word we can use to describe the imposition of fear in the realm of culture—the fear of freedom and with it the fear of *feeling*—is *Philistinism*.

In order to make what I mean clear, I'll share a little personal experience. I was in Berlin, and even though the city was destroyed, I felt a kind of comfort and ease there. Although I was behind the Iron Curtain, and although this was the week the Korean War had started, walking around the American and British section of Berlin I got some sense of what the city had been before it was destroyed. I got a sense of a very comfortable *burgher* kind of life. And I contrasted that sense with how I often feel when I've been in Paris, which is a very beautiful city; how often I feel agitated, and I didn't feel that in Berlin—even though it might be argued that being in Berlin was dangerous and that being in Paris is not. I thought about that and it occurred to me that you have there the essence of the question of Philistinism—anything beautiful, singular, rare, anything that really can touch our feelings can be agitating. Something comfortable and easy, conventional—that does not agitate. And that, in substance, is the reason why Philistines have attacked culture and art.

A very interesting book, although it is basically authoritarian and defends censorship, for example—but a book with many insights—is Leon Trotsky's *Literature and Revolution*. At one point Trotsky had this to say: that it is very difficult to reconstruct one's personality scientifically on the basis of childhood impressions, and that is why many people are revolutionary in theory and Philistine in feeling. You can change that to "liberal" in theory and Philistine in feeling, and it still remains a good insight. There is a tendency in many people to use liberal words, to hail freedom; there is a tendency to glow over art, to pay lip service to its function, but then, at the same time, to attack it, to censor it and to limit the artist and with the artist the original thinker, sometimes by police methods and sometimes by methods of moral intimidation.

Today, the freest form of expression is the book. The book has a very important function to perform. It is literally the only place where a man can, with relative confidence, work out completely his ideas or his feelings in a fictional or non-fictional work and tell all that he needs to tell, develop all and do it with a feeling that what he says will not be censored by the publisher. In newspapers, in most of the magazines and in radio and on television, that is not possible. Among other things, there is not the space; besides the fact that there are many sacred cows and certain restrictions, there is not the space. Also, we have the phenomenon of bigness and mass production. We have a kind of catering to mass tastes or what are believed to be mass tastes. Now, just at the time when a book plays such a vital role, vital for the maintenance and implementation in us of freedom of expression, we have a series of attacks upon it. We have police actions taken in many parts of the United States, and the city of Detroit is now likely to become the new Boston. You know, for years people used to laugh and say about a book, "Was it suppressed in Boston?" Censorship in Boston was a standard joke that goes back to the 1920's. Well, the police department of Detroit draws up lists of books and tells booksellers in advance that they dare not sell those books and that if they do, they will be arrested.

Similar attempts have been made in other parts of the country. I have had some experience with this. Books of mine were seized in Philadelphia in 1947, and we sued the police and got a permanent injunction against them. There were two court cases, and in one of those cases there was a Methodist minister who during the first days of the hearing told me that he was praying for me. I told him that I appreciated his prayers but that he was causing me enough trouble and was violating the Constitution as well, and that I thought he ought to act differently rather than offer prayers. Well, during three days of court hearings, he became increasingly friendly. On the last day, he walked up to me and said: "Mr. Farrell, I think you're a genius, and I wouldn't want your books to be suppressed except that they're sold at twenty-five cents and read by people who shouldn't read them. If they were more expensive, I wouldn't oppose you." This expresses, among other things, a snobbish attitude in censors: If you've got the price of a book costing $2.50 or $3.50, your soul won't be ruined by it; you won't rush off to the nearest brothel and you won't get drunk and you'll be too old to become a juvenile delinquent. You're okay; you're not a problem. But if you pay a quarter for a book, you're in danger of becoming a problem of any number of kinds.

Now, who's afraid here, and who's afraid of what? If we are to have a free society, one of the most important freedoms is the freedom to choose what you want to read—the freedom of access to knowledge. Without access to knowledge, there cannot be growth; people cannot attempt to attain their full stature. Again, we see this most clearly illustrated in the conditions that exist behind the Iron Curtain where there *is* no access to knowledge and where, with great literacy among the people and with hundreds and thousands of newspapers, magazines, pamphlets and books, for a number of years there was only one author. He had many pseudonyms, but he was the only author and the only man who thought. His name was Joseph Stalin. In the Ukraine and most other parts of Russia, according to translations and reports, it was very clear that there was nothing else to contemplate but what he thought, so that today the Russian people are completely uninformed and ignorant of what goes on in the outside world. There is no public opinion to act as a check on any of the policies or actions of the government; the result is that leaders of the government can murder anyone they want, as they have done—Stalin murdered his closest, and boyhood, friend; and there was no way for anybody to protest, unless he too wanted to be murdered. The example of Soviet totalitarianism clearly emphasizes, reveals and dramatizes the importance of freedom of expression—freedom of the expression of ideas, freedom of art, freedom of literature.

I would like to make one further point here. We are in great danger of this thing happening at the present time: that no distinction will be made between, on the one hand, conspiracy—and I would describe the international Communist movement as nothing less than a conspiracy against the human race—and on the other hand heresy and unorthodoxy and originality of thought. The same kinds of attitudes that are now directed against some liberal thinkers, some writers who definitely and clearly are not Communists and are not conspirators, are much similar to the attacks on Walt Whitman, who died a lonely, sick old man, unrecognized by most in his own time and considered immoral by many others. Walt Whitman was a great prophet of freedom, a great poet of freedom and individuality. Today he is read in classrooms. No one has ever given any evidence to show that he has demoralized the United States or that the legacy he left is dangerous. But that attitude which we will call a combination of Philistinism and Know-Nothingism, the latter being a malignant parochialism—that attitude is rampant. It is growing; and frequently it adduces and offers arguments to say that people are incapable of freedom or do not want it. Well, people do not want freedom if they are terrorized or affrighted out of it. And the phenomenon that we call McCarthyism— the efforts of many who are not making a genuine fight against Communism but rather using it as a drive for personal power—constitutes a serious menace to our civil liberties. It is a source of increasing paralysis in this country. Just as when Hitler rose, we now hear many people say that people want only security, they don't want freedom. This is not so. The fear of freedom is basically and fundamentally a condition that is imposed; it is a condition that is imposed in order to satisfy the dictatorial interests of some persons or groups.

In conclusion, let me paraphrase a wonderful insight of Lucretius in *De Rerum Natura*. He says that when a man will cheat and murder and kill for power he evinces a fear of death. The fear of freedom is perhaps linked with a fear of death, and it can be terrible. It can be terrible to die. It can be terrible to make the effort. But the price of freedom is less than the price of tyranny and the price of totalitarianism. If the history of the twentieth century means anything, it means that.

In April, 1917, Lenin said that Russia was the freest country in the world; and this was probably true. In October the Bolsheviks overthrew the Karensky regime and then moved on to create and impose the most terrible tyranny in the history of mankind. In 1933 the Weimar Republic was overthrown and replaced by the National Socialist, or Nazi, Party, and that led to the bloodiest and bitterest war in history. The price of false security, the cost of fear, is shown in all that has flown out of and all that has followed from the international and internal policies of these two dictatorial regimes, regimes that are quite like twin phenomena.

I quoted Whitman and Lincoln at the beginning of this lecture; and I requote Lincoln now: America is the last, best hope of Democracy.

The Middle East in Relationship to The Idea of Freedom and the State

Speech delivered at Miami University,
Oxford, Ohio, March 15, 1957

I want to begin this lecture by reading a passage. It's the conclusion of one of the great books on democracy, and I would recommend that all of you who have not read it, read it. It's Alexis de Tocqueville's *Democracy in America*. At the end of the book, he states, and I quote:

"Providence has not created mankind entirely independent or entirely free. It is true that around every man a fatal circle is traced, beyond which he cannot pass. And within the wide range of that circle, he is powerful and free—so it is with men, and so with communities. The nations of our time cannot prevent the conditions of man from becoming equal, but it depends upon themselves . . . whether the principle of equality is to lead them to servitude or freedom—to knowledge or barbarism, to prosperity or wretchedness."

That was written in the decade before 1848, at which time there were democratic revolutions in Europe. And as a matter of fact, failure of the democratic revolution in Germany is one of the factors that led to Prussianism, autocracy and also, indirectly, was part of the historical background of Hitler. It was the 1848 revolutions that once again stamped the sinister role of Russia on Europe, on world politics—the role of Russia as the enemy of freedom. The shadow of the Tsar hung over Europe at that time. Karl Marx recognized this and spoke of the dangers of Russian imperialism. However, by about the 1870's it was generally believed in the Western world that democracy was the triumphant system and that autocracy was a system in decline; that the future of man in the free world was secure. The late Charles Harrison—I believe his book is called *Political Theories*—mentions this, and points out how this attitude was carried in the West and how it can no longer be accepted.

Now, in the 1880's there was the extensive development of the phenomenon that we call imperialism. When Tocqueville was writing about America as a new world, when men were thinking about the problems of freedom, there had been very little thought given to Asia and Africa, to the countries where today there are new nations. At the same time, it was also believed by many people in the world, and by many thinking people, that the "Jewish problem" had just about been solved. In the 1880's and 1890's in Russia, however, there were pogroms. In France, the most civilized country in the world—in Paris, the center of light, the Athens of the modern world—there was the Dreyfus case, in which General Dreyfus, an obscure and mediocre officer, was named as a traitor to France because he was a wealthy Jew. Crowds marched through the streets of Paris shouting "Death to the Jews." There was a Viennese journalist in Paris at the time—very clever, and possibly a great man—named Theodor Herzl. Theodor Herzl drew the conclusion that if this was the attitude toward Jews in Paris, then Jews everywhere must have their own homeland; and as a consequence, Herzl was the organizer of the first World Zionist Congress in Basel in 1897. He wrote in one of his diaries—which are, incidentally, remarkable books; they have recently been republished here and I would recommend them to you—that, at the end of the conference, he had said, "Today I've founded the Jewish state." He said that within fifty years there would be a Jewish state in Palestine, and he anticipated not only the year—fifty years after Herzl made that prophecy, on May 14, 1948, a Jewish state was founded—but also the character of the state. With that, the Zionist movement developed.

The Zionist movement was not purely a religious movement, and it was not purely a nationalist movement, in the sense of nationalism without social content. There were various wings of Zionism. One wing was that of the Labor Zionists, who went to Palestine in the 1900's to work the land. This is called the Second Allyah. One of the men of the Second Allyah was David Ben-Gurion. As late as 1907, Ben-Gurion called for admission of the Labor Zionists to the Second Socialist International.

The Labor Zionists, while deeply conscious of themselves as Jews, were also socialists. The ideas of socialism, which were the ideas and hopes of the Russian Revolution, excited them. Prior to the Bolshevik Revolution, and to the subsequent degeneration of a tradition and a movement into one of the most vicious and terrible totalitarianisms in history, socialism was regarded as the hope of Europe. The moral contribution that socialism made to the life of Europe before the First World War cannot be calculated; it cannot be overestimated. And the ideas of freedom and progress that were associated with socialism had stirred Russia ever since the Napoleonic invasion. At the same time the Labor Zionists were impressed by, influenced by, stirred and roused by the ideas and aims of the Russian revolutionary movement.

Now with these historical remarks in mind, I want to paraphrase a sentence from another book that I would recommend to you, *The Revolt of the Masses*, by Ortega y Gassett. At one point in that book Gassett remarks that the state is a creation. I think that we should recognize that the state and society are creations—of the mind, of thought, of imagination, of the moral sense, the skill, the labor and the muscle of men and women of many generations. The state is not something that grows to us naturally. And it is through the state and through society that we gain many things that are assumed to be natural—our name, our status, our sense of identification. All of these are considerably a consequence of the state and of the kind of state we have, and I think you might gain a sense of this if you read two novels of Kafka— *The Trial* and *The Castle*. His character, Mr. K., does not have a name—he does not have status, home, identity. In *The Trial*, he's going to be tried and found guilty, but he doesn't know what he's going to be tried for. There is a kind of frightening hallucinatory character to Kafka's work. All that we accept as natural and part of our identity is questioned or virtually nonexistent in the Kafkalian world. Some critics, among them William Phillips, an editor of the *Partisan Review*, describe Kafka as having pictured a spiritualized bureaucracy.

We must recognize, then, that there is tradition and continuity in society, and that tradition is the product of many generations—the product of a long history, and of much thought, and of much suffering. Since the Renaissance, and particularly since the American colonial revolution and the great French Revolution, the drive for equality has gone on steadily in the world. The developments of technology have made equality and a higher standard of living more practicable. They have also created many new problems concerning democracy. For instance, the traditional view of democracy was that the government is best which governs least. Today those who are most democratic in their thinking are among the advocates of more government, of the larger role of government in society. And those who are conservative and less democratic in their thinking assert and defend the original ideas of democracy. In America, this struggle was focused in the writings of two of our greatest founding fathers—Alexander Hamilton and Thomas Jefferson. The democrats are more Hamiltonian today and, in a sense, the conservatives are more Jeffersonian.

After the end of the Second World War, as you all know, many new nations were created, and with that we have the phenomenon of nationalism. In passing, many people today think that nationalism *per se* is necessarily good and necessarily healthy. Senator Hubert H. Humphrey, a Democratic liberal and perhaps one of the best Senators in the

U.S. Senate, was recently quoted in the press, in reference to the crimes and the serious danger in the Middle East, as saying that, "Of course, this is a manifestation of nationalism, and nationalism is healthy." I think that he was very thoughtless in making that remark. The American historian, the late Carlton J. Hayes, said that nationalism was the religion of the nineteenth century; but there are various kinds of nationalism. There was, and is, a strong element of nationalism in Zionism. But nationalism involves a question of social content, too.

It is important to think of this today, and particularly in relationship to the new countries of Asia. Now, many Americans assume that these new countries are at the stage at which the United States was when the thirteen colonies became a nation; that assumption is wrong, and it is wrong in many ways. It is wrong because these nations are, in the main, hundreds of years behind where the citizens and the inhabitants of the thirteen colonies were in the year 1776, when the Declaration of Independence was proclaimed. This is true of virtually all of these nations except Japan and Israel. On the other hand, while these countries are backward and underdeveloped (even though, in passing, Prime Minister Nehru of India once said in one of my interviews with him that it is humiliating to these nations to continue to talk of their underdevelopment)—while these countries are backward, they have their own traditions and religions, and these are different from those of the past in the West. I put this question to Nehru. I said that it was debatable whether the United States had anything to contribute to India that would be valuable in the face of its overwhelming problems, and I mentioned that the social relationships that existed in Russia before the two revolutions of 1917 and the social relationships of China before the success of the Chinese Communists in 1949 were more like the social relationships of India; and the economic problems of India were more like the economic problems faced following the revolutions in China and Russia than like conditions in the West and especially in the United States. When I put these things to Nehru, I had this in mind: To a considerable extent, the Asians can get techniques and know-how from Japan, from Russia and, to some degree, from China—or they will be able to get them from China in ten or twenty years. American know-how, American technique, while in many ways superior to those of other countries, is not absolutely and vitally necessary for the development of India, Indonesia, Pakistan and the Arab countries; as a matter of fact, right now and in the years to come, there are many Japanese technologists and statisticians and others who have been and will be supplied to the new Asian countries. For example, when I was in Pakistan I went to a large textile factory where there were mills, or machines, almost as large as this room, and these machines came from many countries of the world. When I talked to the manager, I discovered that in his office was a group of Japanese, who were going over his books and studying the way that he conducted his business. I had this in mind when I spoke to Nehru, and he answered that there was one thing to consider: There was freedom. He said that of course freedom existed in very few countries in the world. He mentioned the Scandinavian countries and France and England; he didn't mention the United States in that context at all, and he said that he didn't consider West Germany free, in which I think he was wrong. He asked, "Do you think that there is any freedom in the Arab world?" meaning, I think, freedom in the sense we can briefly describe as the ideas of Liberty, Equality and Fraternity; the ideas of individualism and faith in the role of reason, and the belief that the best kind of society that can be established is one in which rights exist for citizens. Now these ideas *have* come to backward Asian countries that until only a few years ago were colonies of imperialist Western nations, and they *are* a product of the West, and they cause conflict. They bring on a clash of traditions; for instance, in Pakistan there is a great deal of thinking about democracy and personality in relation to Islam. In the traditions of Islam, the revered poet-philosopher of Pakistan, Iqbal, was one of the Western exponents. He believed that the influences of the West should be felt in the Moslem world, and at the same time he studied all of the philosophers—the Western philosophers, both the medieval ones and the modern ones, and he criticized every one of them, including those who have a direct relationship to democracy, such as Kant. And the two philosophers whom he praised were St. Thomas Aquinas, the great philosopher of the medieval system, and the twentieth century philosopher, Max Shaler, who believed that philosophy was a form of class struggle. He was a mystic, and more or less a religious thinker. That should reveal concretely what I mean—that the ideas of the West must be and are in conflict with the ideas, the traditions and the religions of these countries.

Things will be different in fifty years. The terrible barriers of poverty will probably be broken. At the present time in India there are something like seventy-nine million unemployed and underemployed. The underemployed are those who cannot earn enough money to have a subsistence level of existence. In Pakistan there are refugee camps of Moslems who left India when the crown colony of India was partitioned into the present states of India and Pakistan, and those refugee camps by the bay are as horrible as anything I have ever seen. But while living in squalor it is possible to have a roof over your

24

head in the factory, and it is even possible to work in an air-conditioned factory. And the Asians are learning industrial techniques—they're producing goods, driving tanks, driving airplanes and even developing Western knowledge of statistics. For instance, one of the remarkable documents of Asia in the present period is the Second Indian Five Points Plan; anyone who goes through it can see the degree to which the Indians are beginning to master statistical economics. But the question is: Is this development? Is this a drive toward freedom and equality? While there are many remnants of the caste system in India, there *is* a drive toward equality. Women are more free. In the recent elections, there was a boy of twenty-one, of very low status. I believe he was called a *Chaprasi*; he was one of those who stand outside the door of a distinguished person and run errands for him. He decided he wanted to be a member of Parliament, and he was elected in Bombay. But the question remains—is the drive toward equality, is the conquest of backwardness, is the conquest of misery—misery, the likeness of which does not exist in any part of the U.S. or Europe outside the Iron Curtain, with the possible exception of Greece and Spain—is all of this going to be carried out under conditions of servitude or freedom?

Although the Indians won't admit it, one of the central facts of Asia today is the competition for the soul of Asia that goes on between India and China. Some of the Indians even envy the Chinese. They envy them because, having a totalitarian system and a police state, the Chinese can manage masses of people more easily, and in doing so, can concentrate work forces; whereas the Indians, who are trying under difficult conditions to establish and maintain a democracy, cannot. There have been many criticisms of the Indian Second Five Year Plan, on the grounds that it will lead to totalitarianism and on the grounds that there is a danger of the state becoming too important in the economic life of the country. This is a serious danger. There are about two to three million trade-union members in India, divided into three unions, one of which is Communist. And there are 360 million or so people in India. The major trade union is actually an auxiliary of the Congress Party, and is financed by the Congress Party. The government of India is taking an ever larger role in the economy. In the five-year plans and in the writings about Indian traditions, they talk of the public and the private sectors in economy. But there is only one privately owned, modernized, efficient steel plant, the Tata Works.

Prior to the present, there have not been many capitalists in India, in the sense that there are capitalists in the U.S. There were not trained people who would organize and manage industry and money, and there is not the same amount of free capital that there is here; those who were capitalists were largely merchants and largely made their living through and along with the imperialists of the country who ruled them—England. Today, if the development of India were left to free enterprise in the sense that it is left to free enterprise in the U.S., India probably could not develop. There has to be an allocation of capital, and there has to be much planning, or a country as large and as backward as India could not even hope to break the barriers of poverty. Even so, one of the officials of the Indian government to whom I spoke stated that it will probably be twenty years yet before the gains made will overcome the increase in Indian population. He said that he hoped that, at the end of the third five-year plan, some of the textile workers of India would, perhaps, make the equivalent of $180 a year in American money.

Now, there are many other problems that can be seen in these countries. There is no public opinion in the sense that we know it in the West. Much communication has to be oral, through speeches and through the radio—an important fact to keep in mind in connection with the Arab world, and with the present power of the dictator of the Nile, Colonel Nasser. Also, these countries are not nations. They are aspiring to be nations. In India, there are sixteen languages, and there is much hatred and distrust among the various linguistic groups. For instance, in January of 1955, I believe it was, over 670 people were murdered in the brutal riots in Bombay. When I was in Bombay there were other riots and there were more people killed. And if anybody is interested in becoming a commissioner of riots, I suggest he go to India. The riots of Paris or New York are civilized in comparison. Indian riots probably compare only with what I've read of the riots of the Gaza Strip and the Cairo street crowds. The Maharajah-speaking groups will begin by wanting to throw stones at the police and at other linguistic groups, they'll end by throwing stones at anybody and everybody, at themselves, at their wives . . . . They just go wild. It's an unreasoning, violent, terrible wildness and destructiveness. In one riot in India, the strikers dropped an engineer from an engine and let the engine run right into a crowd of people. It's the hatred and misery of frustration that causes these things. And one of the prime dangers to Indian democracy is that it will be destroyed by mob violence.

The point to be made here is this: When we consider the question of democracy, when we consider the growth of tradition, when we consider the organization of society toward freedom, the size of a country has much to do with it. The problems of India are magnified many times because of its size. In contrast it is easy to have democracy in smaller countries, such as Holland and Denmark and Israel.

Now, if we look at democracy as an experiment, I would say that among new nations India and Israel can be called the great experiments in democracy of our time. It is easiest and best to go to Israel, if one is going, after one has come from Asia. When I flew from the airport in Jerusalem to Tel Aviv and then to Paris I was flying over Greece, Italy and parts of France, and I happened to think how large Italy seems in comparison with Israel. . . . You can fly across Israel in a few minutes. Eight thousand square kilometers constitute the entire country. News of the Arab-Israeli conflict, which was already becoming tense with daily infiltrations when I left, was front-page news in the English and French-speaking press of Israel, as was the Suez crisis which had already erupted; but when I got to Paris and Nasser seized the canal, Israel and her crises received only *that* much space. It's a little country. But it's a country with the highest standard of living of any in Asia, and it is different from other Asian countries, too, in that it is a Western country, and a democratic country. It is a country that is a bridge from East to West and West to East, one which could make a tremendous contribution to the area of Asia in which it exists; but which is not wanted as a bridge very much by the West, and which the neighboring Arab states want to destroy—to exterminate, and drive every Israeli Jew, 1,600,000 of them, into the sea.

I mentioned Theodor Herzl. When the Jews began to return to Israel, and especially from 1900 on, they did so to work the land. The original purchases of land were made by the Baron de Rothschild and the Baron de Hirsch. But these did not work out, and the Jewish Agency, in connection with the Zionist movement, was established and bought land to be worked. It bought sub-marginal land—malaria-infected marshes, land that was rocky and that had suffered erosion and the neglect of centuries, land that had been allowed to erode since the time of the Romans. Jewish settlers had to develop their own institutions. At that time, Palestine was ruled by the Ottoman Turkish Empire. There was little medicine. There were few doctors. Work had to be made; work had to be collective and cooperative. Settlers had to defend themselves.

Ben-Gurion was one of those who went to Palestine. He went to be a farm worker, and he was the man who urged the Jewish settlers to hire their own watchmen and guards, rather than depend on the Arabs to protect them from marauders, theft, violence and destruction of property. If you read *Time*, you may have read a story about Ben-Gurion a week or two ago, in which he was called the "Old Watchman," meaning an old-time guard of the settlers. Out of this situation there developed a defense force. There developed a number of other singular and peculiar institutions too. One was the *kibbutz*. It is declining in importance today, but it was one of the significant institutions in the development of what has become modern Israel. And it made a significant contribution to raising the level of production in that area, which is mighty important.

The first *kibbutz* was established in 1909. The *kibbutz* can be looked at in different ways, but the first thing to think of in connection with *kibbutzim* is a phrase of Karl Marx, "the idiocy of rural life." Think of what it would have meant for individual farmers to work on eroded, rocky land without cooperation to redeem it, to protect themselves and to market their crops. So, the *kibbutz* is a communal institution. Everyone is equal and no one earns any money. All needs are taken care of, and a small sum of money is yearly given to each of the members. *Kibbutzim* are run democratically. The manager or coordinator of work, which is the most unpopular job, is elected. For a long time none of the members of *kibbutzim* wanted the office jobs, the directing jobs; they wanted to work in the fields, to do agricultural labor. I mentioned pre-World-War-One socialism and the Russian Revolution, and the *kibbutz* is, to some degree, a product of those times. In 1920, the representatives of four thousand Israeli workers met in Haifa and founded the General Confederation of Jewish Workers, which is called the *Histadrut*. I want to emphasize the fact that work had to be *made*. These workers would one day do work on the roads, the next day in the fields. So the confederation that was formed was not one in which the worker joined a specific union, as happens in the United States, where we have the AF of L and the CIO, and as is the case in most countries. The worker had to join the whole Workers' Confederation. Later on, as *Histadrut* grew, there were established individual unions. But work had still to be made, because there was continuing immigration, and so the *Histadrut* went into business; and today, besides being a trade-union organization, it runs factories and markets, has a village of its own and has organized and directs a subsidiary organization, the *Kopput Holim*, which is the entire health program of the Israelis—and it's a remarkable health program, particularly considering the fact that Israel is a poor country. Also the *Histadrut* has taken in and is taking in Arab workers. For a long time, the Jews felt that it was best for there to be separate Arab unions, and there were two. One of them was called the Palestinian Labor League. It was opposed by many of the Arab leaders, and today, *Histadrut* has created an Arab department, and every Arab worker in Israel is eligible—except, I believe, any Arab who owns more than forty-eight dun-bans of land, which is about fifteen or so acres; but he can join a cooperative. No one who employs others can belong to *Histadrut*. Housewives are members, and all members of government belong. As a matter of fact, Ben-Gurion at one time was Labor Secretary of *Histadrut*; and so, I believe, was the present foreign minister of Israel, Mrs. Golda Meir, who used to be a schoolteacher. In passing, the salaries of Arab teachers in Israel are now equal to those of Jewish teachers. In the period of the British mandate, the Jews established their own schools, and their wages were higher than wages in Arab schools.

I mentioned the British mandate—that is, after the First World War, Palestine was ruled by Britain under a mandate given to it by the now-defunct League of Nations. Now, in 1947 the Security Council of the United Nations passed a resolution providing for the partitioning of Palestine into a Jewish and an Arab state, which would exist together in economic union. From then tension and fighting began. The British left Palestine on May 14, 1948. On the night of May 14th, the state of Israel was proclaimed. On the morning of May 15th, the armies of five Arab nations marched into Israel. At five in the morning of the day after Israel was proclaimed, Tel-Aviv, where the proclamation was read, was bombed for the first time. Jerusalem was cut off. The Israelis had no army; they had only a defense force. When the British general was leaving Israel, he said to his Jewish friends in Haifa, "I'll see you all in Hell." He expected the Arabs to win the war in a week or two. Some of the Arab leaders proclaimed it was a holy war; one of them said that there would be butchery the like of which had not happened since the time of Genghis Khan. And to the surprise of everybody but themselves, the Israeli Jews defeated five Arab armies. The Egyptians marched across the Gaza strip and were finally surrounded on the road that runs parallel to the Gaza strip in Israeli territory. The general of the Israeli forces—by this time, Israel had an army—was an archeologist named Allon, who is now one of the leaders of the extreme left. As a consequence of his archeological studies and his readings of the Bible, he recalled roads that were unknown to the Arabs, and he led his troops through these roads to surround and conquer the Egyptians. General Allon felt that it was useless and needless to continue the slaughter once his forces actually had won, and since he wanted to employ his forces elsewhere he decided to have armistice talks with the Egyptians. A Yemenite Jew, a Captain Cohen, went across the battle line with a white flag in one hand and his other hand at his holster. He and the Egyptian general arranged for armistice talks, which were held just inside the Israeli line.

Now, one of the officers—and, the Israelis say, a brave one—on the

Egyptian staff was a man named Gamal Abdel Nasser, and Nasser and Cohen became friends as a consequence of the talks. There is an article Captain Cohen wrote in the February 23, 1953 issue of a London magazine called the *Jewish Observer*, titled "The Secret Armistice Talks in Negeb," in which Cohen tells the story of the talks. Cohen points out that Nasser felt the Egyptians were fighting the wrong war in fighting Israel; that their war was the revolutionary war at home against King Farouk and foreign domination. Cohen claims that other Egyptian officers felt bitter and betrayed as well, and Nasser confirms this in his book, *Egypt's Liberation*. Cohen also pointed out to some of his fellow Israeli officers that the Jews had fought against British imperialism and that they had attempted to arouse the moral conscience of the world.

At the talks, the Egyptian officers questioned the Israelis a great deal about their institutions, such as the *kibbutz*. They had dinner at a *kibbutz*, and after that, when fighting was resumed and the Egyptian general was not allowed to surrender by his government in Egypt—the government of King Farouk—the Egyptians were captured and beaten. The Egyptian general gave specific instructions not to bombard with the Egyptian artillery the particular *kibbutz* at which the officers had eaten. The last thing that Nasser said to Captain Cohen was, "I'll see you in Egypt." When Nasser became ruler of Egypt, the Israelis hoped that this might lead to peace. Now, when Nasser's book, *Egypt's Liberation*—and it is a book which, in my opinion, makes *Mein Kampf* look something like a work of genius—first appeared in America, Walter Lippman wrote a column in which he made a very obvious, or not obvious but a very clear and perceptive and fair judgment upon it, pointing out this: that the tragedy of Egypt is a result of the fact that the national revolution came at a time when the need for social reform was so imperative. I mentioned before that we must recognize that there are different kinds of nationalism and that all nationalism cannot be considered equal. Although Egypt is a large country—with, I believe, something like 130,000 square miles of habitable land—the infant mortality rate, according to the last figures published ten years ago, was 250 per thousand. Prior to the seizing of the Suez Canal—the crises, the war, the blocking of Egyptian funds—Egypt annually imported about one hundred million dollars more than it exported in goods. Cotton made up about 80 per cent of its exports. There is great illiteracy in Egypt, and the life span is something like thirty-six years.

I happened to run into Captain Cohen by accident in Tel Aviv. Although we didn't talk about the article, he did say, "I know Nasser.

He's an honest man. He's too big for his boots, however, and he's politically inexperienced." Now, I think that the book *Egypt's Liberation will* reveal a lack of political experience, in the sense of the concepts and developments, etc., of world politics. It is a difficult thing, particularly with Russian backing and the Suez Canal as blackmail, to have flexible tactics, and especially easy, when you have Nazi advisors in your government, to do as the Egyptian government has done. Egypt has one of the weakest economies in the world—it's a weaker economy than India's—and a road of foreign aggrandizement, a glorification of a dictator, is easier than to tackle this problem.

Now, the Arab-Israeli problem is not the only problem in the Middle East, and as a matter of fact one of the serious problems is an intense fight for power and a drive for unity among the many Arab states. There are different levels of Arab states; some, the oil-producing ones, are rich. The others are poor. Lebanon, a small and very attractive country, is the freest and perhaps the most civilized and Westernized of the Arab countries. In Saudi Arabia, as we read in the paper, slaves are owned and thieves have their hands chopped off if they are caught stealing. . . . There is much difference. And the struggle for Arab unity and the struggle for power are focused in the rivalry of Iraq and Egypt. Among the newly emerging Arab groups are young intellectuals and army officers, and they are the main Nasserites. Now, they grew up in the era of Stalin, Hitler and Mussolini. They gained their ideas of the West at a time when the West was in decay. I mentioned Ben-Gurion's generation and something of the significance to it of the socialist movement in Europe prior to 1914 and of the Russian revolution. The West that Ben-Gurion represents is a West in a period of hope and confidence and freedom. The West that has influenced many of these evolving and developing nations is a West of decay and totalitarianism, and this, I think, is one aspect of the situation that has not been sufficiently commented upon.

With all of these remarks in mind, I want to draw a few simple conclusions. I want to raise these points: First, we must remember that democracy is a product of the effort of men, that democracy demands skill, intelligence and effort, and that day by day it must be created and, in a sense, recreated by the citizens of a democracy. Second, in many new nations, we have unfertile conditions for Western democracy, and this for various reasons. For instance, in Indonesia, which is now in a state almost of anarchy, there are three thousand islands on which eighty million people live; but when the Dutch left, I believe there were only something like two hundred and fifty doctors and fifty Indonesian engineers. Even today the Indonesians do not have

31

enough people trained to make a government effective. When I was in Indonesia and tried to cash a check, the way they'd look at the check, and the way some of them would look at my passport when I applied to get an exit permit, made me think of high-school students who were trying to learn to read.

India is different from Indonesia; one of the reasons why India has a chance is because the British trained a civil service. Despite all that is said against imperialism—and it is not my intention here to defend it—everything about imperialism is not positively bad, and particularly in the case of the English. The English having left a well-trained civil service, India was in the position to make the effort to be a democratic society. Although I do not at all agree with the foreign policy of the Indian government, I want to emphasize that, internally, India is a democratic country, and that its government and its leaders are working as hard as they can to maintain a line of democracy; and I think that this is very important.

A little while ago I stated that the Western idea of freedom—liberty, equality, fraternity, etc.—comes from the past, and that the carriers of this idea into the East were the imperialists, and that created suspicion. I would like to make a further point that relates to the United States: Most of the new nations of the middle East and Asia are ruled by intellectuals who have had a Western education—French or, more commonly, English, either abroad or in their own countries. The Indian delegate to the United Nations, for example, Mr. V. K. Krishna Menon, whom I have read about and heard read his speeches on TV, could be described as virtually an English Bevinite. As everybody knows, for some generations there have been a number of English and European clichés about America—that America is a second-rate civilization and so on; and these ideas were absorbed by many of the present rulers of Asia, who, in learning of the West, more or less conceived a contempt for America and Americans. The United States is the richest and most powerful country in the world, and when the United States talks of freedom its talk is met with suspicion, because the freedom that these countries want, or half want, is regarded also as the product of their former masters. Under these circumstances, I think we should recognize this: that our ideas of freedom and democracy are a challenge to these people and create in them a condition of conflict, and that our ideas must be tested against the ideas and traditions and religions native to the Middle East and Asia in order to be assimilated at all.

This is my third point: Along with backwardness, with misery and poverty, there is a great impatience for progress, and this impatience for progress can have the effect of leading the East to attempt totalitarian methods. That is one of the criticisms of Nehru by some of the Indians opposed to him. And we can see the same tendency in present events in Indonesia, where Sukarno was attempting to establish a controlled democracy and where it became very clear that he was more impressed by the political ideas and the system he saw in China and the Soviet Union than he was after his visit to the United States.

Now, I should have liked to talk about one more thing, but I have taken up too much of your time. That thing would have been new immigrants into Israel. There are over four hundred thousand of them who are from Oriental and African countries. Over two hundred thousand of them are from Arab countries. In the experience of new immigrants, in their reactions to their new land and in how they develop, one perceives a kind of living anthropology, a sharp illustration of some of the conditions and conflicts in the whole question of East and West.

Finally, with all the foregoing remarks in mind, I shall quote from *Freedom and Culture* by the late John Dewey: "If there is one conclusion to which human experience unmistakably points, it is that democratic ends demand democratic methods for their realization. Authoritarian ends now offer themselves to us in new guises." I believe this to be true, and that it is one of the roots of the world's problems today.

I do not have any final or absolute conclusions to make here, but I shall state that I think and that the sense of my lecture has been this: that these are aspects of some of the problems that not only we, but the world, face today. Some of the ideas that I have expressed here I had long before I took this trip around the world; but much that I have seen has emphasized and proved that they are at least warrantable, and in this sense, worth considering.

Problems of Becoming a Writer

Speech delivered at Seattle University, April 17, 1956

I said I would talk of problems of the writer. I will begin by saying that there are a number of misleading notions about writing and writers, and a number of confusions. Some people think that a writer's life is always one of great adventure, great excitement. There may be excitement and moments of adventure in the life of a writer; but as a writer, what he does is to sit down by himself, usually in a room alone, and spend hours upon endless hours trying to put onto the paper something of what he sees, something of what he feels, something of what he knows and something of what he imagines about what is our common human experience.

I believe that a fundamental reason why people write is the need for expression. There are other reasons: the need for fame; the desire—a curious vanity that exists in all men and that exists very strongly in writers—to speak beyond the grave; the desire for money or reward. All of these things go into making the motivation of a writer. But what is fundamental is the need for expression. The need for expression is also a need for communication; it is a need for the sharing of experience. John Dewey, the great American philosopher and educator, was of the view that the highest human good, which is called the "summum bonum" in works of philosophy and ethics, is shared experience. Writing is a form of shared experience.

A much misunderstood book is Leo Tolstoy's book, *What Is Art?* When Tolstoy wrote it he had already changed from his earlier views, and in it he attacked much of the literature and art of the West. He attacked it because he was of the opinion that it could not be understood and appreciated by a simple, and in many instances an illiterate, Russian peasantry. But even though Tolstoy was often so perceptive, so incisive, so clear in his understanding, he was sometimes quite wrongheaded; he was most obviously wrong-headed in this thesis. Still, there are many insights in this book. At one point he tells us, and I am paraphrasing, that thanks to human culture it is possible to know all that has been thought and felt in the past and all that is being thought and felt in the present; and through the rendition of what is thought and felt in art, we become infected with emotion. Now, maybe we

34

cannot know *all* that is thought and felt, but we can know something of what is thought and felt, and all of us need to give expression to what we know, in one form or another.

What a writer does is to take the common features of our day-by-day experience and work them out. In the course of a day, all of us have innumerable fantasies and dreams, or fragments and snatches of dreams, both conscious and unconscious. We have curiosities, moments of exaltation and moments of despair, moments when we feel proud of ourselves and moments of guilt and shame. Through our consciousness in the course of any day, waking and sleeping, the elements of from six to ten or more lifetimes come and go in fragments. A writer takes one of these—takes a curiosity, a feeling, an experience or an episode—and he works it out in detail—in some detail if he's writing a short story, in greater detail if he's writing a novel—and then develops it.

There are four lines in a poem of the nineteenth-century French poet, Rimbaud, which I will quote in translation: "The wolf cries out under the trees and regurgitates on the gorgeous feathers of the fouls which he has eaten. Like him I consume myself." It's a very rough translation, from memory. Rimbaud, as you know, was a brilliant and highly complicated poet and was one of the founders of the Symbolist movement in French literature, and his poetry is far, far removed from a literature of the common person. But at the same time, if you take what is being expressed in those four lines of poetry—idealism, revulsion at having gorged onself and having attained satiety or surfeit, and then the comparison with the wolf and the idea of self-consumption—it becomes clear that feelings like these occur to everyone. An ordinary domestic servant, or even a person who is illiterate, might have the same kind of feelings, although he or she would not express them in the way that Rimbaud has.

So in this sense I would say that the elements, the substance, the material of literature are, is, the common experience all of us go through: the common experience socially and overtly, and internally and personally when we are face to face with ourselves. And because of this I would state that literature is, or should be, a normal part of one's life as well as a normal part of the culture of any time.

Now, if one of the primary motives of the writer is the need for expression, one of the primary problems—perhaps the biggest problem—that a writer faces is that of winning his own self-confidence, of attaining a sufficient amount of inner security so that he feels that he *can* write. At times this is a question of whether he dares to write. The problem is felt most acutely when one is a young writer or is in the first years of a literary career, but it occurs to writers during their entire life-times. I recall a letter of Joseph Conrad. Conrad is not so much read today, but in my estimation he was one of the greatest writers of English of this century. After reading proof, Conrad asked, What is the use? How and why should I write? And in the letters, diaries and biographies of writers one will find again and again references to moments when confidence has waned and seems almost shattered, when the writer feels that it all has been a mistake; when the writer is fearful that he cannot do it. So—and this is addressed particularly to those of you who have the desire to write—do not think that the question of confidence is peculiar to you or that, because of it, there is necessarily something wrong and weak in you.

Of course, the problem of winning one's own confidence is not peculiar to the writer. It's part of what we all have to face. As human beings we have to win some confidence in ourselves, and after having won it we have to keep rewinning it all during our lives. If you have aspirations or ambitions to be something other than a writer, you will very frequently meet with the same doubts and the same need of winning and holding, retaining and rewinning your own confidence. In this sense there is something common as well as special in the problems of a writer.

I would like to make a few remarks on what I will call consciousness or awareness. The problem of awareness or consciousness is acute for a writer, for the obvious reason that while things are happening to him he is driven with the need to grasp them quickly, to understand them and to render them. In "The Cherry Orchard," by Anton Chekhov, there is a character, a writer, named Trigorin, who speaks of this in a moving and eloquent passage. The sense of it is that the writer is at work twenty-four hours a day. He cannot let anything slip by, he must catch as much as he can. He must see, and he must catch what he sees, and he must have the phrases that will permit him to render what he sees so that someone else will be able to understand it. He must create an image in or convey a feeling to the mind of someone else.

Everything I have said so far would, I believe, give strength to the point that writing is, or at least should be regarded as, one of the normal features not only of our life and times but of any life and time, and that the problems of writing and writers are only specific illustrations of the problems of people in general—albeit they are sometimes more internally dramatic or acute than the problems of others, of non-writers; and that the process of becoming a writer and the motives for doing so are similar to the processes and motives of all of us in our efforts to come to terms with our own destinies, to meet our experience and grow, and to live out our individual life cycles.

But there are other matters which can be spoken of in connection with writing. At various times, a society may be more or less hospitable to writing. I wrote a little fable recently, which has not been published, about a writer who became what is referred to as famous. The more famous, or celebrated, he became, the more taxes he had to pay; the more trouble he had. The more trouble he had, the harder he had to work, so that it was endless, until finally he died a premature death and went to the nether world. When he was burning in the flames of hell, he discovered that around him there were clergymen who did not censor books, there were policemen who neither bothered nor arrested writers, there were tax collectors who did not collect taxes, there were critics who did not criticize and there were editors who neither accepted nor rejected a writer. And he found that it was hot in hell and that he was burning pretty fiercely, but apart form the flames it was a free economy and a free society: Nobody bothered you, arrested you, collected taxes from you or in any way tormented you, and perhaps hell was the best place for a writer to be. Because it is a fact that, especially in that vein or category of writing that we call realistic, every generation of writers for at least a century has, at one time or another, won for itself the dubious honor of gaining the solicitations of the police and the courts. In other words, it has had censorship trouble. In the Second Empire of Louis Napoleon, or Napoleon III, Flaubert was hauled into court because of *Madame Bovary*. His novel was exonerated; it was not banned. But his contemporary, the great poet and critic of literature and art, Baudelaire, was brought into court because of his volume of poetry, *Les Fleurs du Mal*, *The Flowers of Evil*, and it was suppressed. In the United States, a library in Brooklyn, I believe it was, would not allow the circulation of Mark Twin's *The Adventures of Huckleberry Finn* because of its attacks upon and lampoons of the institution of royalty. When Leo Tolstoy's *Resurrection*, a novel that is clearly and intensely moral, was translated, it was not allowed to travel through the mails of the United States; it was banned by American postal authorities. For a long time James Joyce's great novel, *Ulysses*, which perhaps has had more influence on the novel and on writers than any other book of this century, was banned by the United States Customs Service. Year in and year out, writers face the same kind of attacks.

More and more often in the United States, however, the censors have been failing. We have had a remarkably good series of court decisions—and we have been getting court decisions for a number of years—exonerating serious works of literature that are considered by some to be immoral, demoralizing, etc., because they attempt frankly and directly to look at and to render certain aspects and features of human experience. But there is still pressure—a pressure that is potential, that is often silent, that many people do not feel, that a number are not aware of, but a pressure that continues to exist in our society and in other countries and that, at times, can be an intimidating factor.

Now, when William James was a young man he wanted to be a painter, but while he was in Paris he decided that he didn't have what it took, and he gave up his ambition to be a painter or a creative artist in order to become a scientist and a teacher. In a letter announcing his decision to a sister, he remarked, "What is worse than a mediocre writer?" Now, I do not want to seem arrogant, and all of us should be a little bit careful in talking about this matter of mediocrity, but I would say the same; if a writer is rendered, or renders himself, or allows himself to be rendered more or less mediocre by pressures in the environment or by outright fears of censorship—and if his sincerity and his willingness to deal frankly with the condition of man is insufficient—then we have an effort that is not worth a candle, because in the first and last analyses it is senseless to fool people by writing lies or even needless ambiguities. It is a waste of time both for the writer and for the reader. There are too many things to do in life, too many other opportunities, so that it would seem to me to be the most senseless thing in the world to lock oneself up in one's room and read some insincere, trivial book.

Besides the pressures of censorship and pressures toward conformity a writer may have to contend with, there is the matter of economics. I might say this—just think how much less feeling for and depth of understanding of ancient Greece we might have if it were not for Euripedes and Aristotle. Think how much less we might know of the end of the medieval period if it were not for Dante, and how much less meaningful the Elizabethan period would be for us but for Shakespeare; think, too, how much less moving we might find, and what a shallower understanding we might have of, what is best and most precious in American freedom and democracy but for their ecstatic celebration by Walt Whitman, who was, perhaps, the first American poet of world stature. This should make clear the need for and the importance of writing. But while there is a need for writing, there is never a certain need for any particular writer, and every new writer must find his own way. His work must find its way. At no time is it likely that he'll be able to feel assured and guaranteed that his way will be quick and easy and that he'll have success, or that if he has success, he will retain it. At no time can the writer feel sure of his future in advance. In writing there is a kind of permanent insecurity. One year a writer may be very successful—he may have a book that has a big sale. The next year he may not be able to finish a book. There may be a change in fashions, in attitudes, in styles. A new generation may come along, and generally speaking, most of the writers of a new generation feel that they are better writers and better, more independent people than their immediate predecessors, and they attack them; so that there will be changes and attacks, and the writer who is most popular and influencial today may be forgotten tomorrow. Those of us who are older recall, for instance, that in the 1920's James Branch Cabell was considered one of the leading American writers. Today he is scarcely spoken of.

I was talking tonight with a friend of mine from Chicago, and we were recalling Finley Peter Dunne, the creator of "Mr. Dooley" for the Chicago *Evening Post*. Finley Peter Dunne is, in my opinion, one of the really great American writers. His Mr. Dooley column used to appear weekly in Chicago and in other newspapers for a number of years; it was read widely at the end of the nineteenth century and the early part of this one. But how many younger people today even know that once there was a great humorous writer by the name of Finley Peter Dunne? In the case of Dunne, obscurity came after his death, but it can happen in one's lifetime.

At the same time, I would say that conditions for writers are much better economically—much better in many ways—in the United States than in any country in the world. In Italy, a good sale for a book is 2,500 to 3,000 copies. In small countries such as Holland, Denmark, Norway and Sweden, which are, by necessity, bilingual and where the learning of a second language is compulsory, the language that is most spoken after the native language is English. Now, on the one hand, because these are small countries and their languages are not well known by many people outside of them, there is a very limited market for native books; on the other hand, because almost everyone in these countries speaks English, there are a large number of English and American books, both fiction and nonfiction, that are read. In Holland, Denmark and Sweden, you'd be amazed by the number of people who know a great deal about American literature and by the number of modern American novels and books of short stories that may have been read.

Now, for a Scandinavian writer, this means that, besides the fact that he has a limited market, he has a good deal of competition from abroad, especially from the United States. In some countries, the Latin American countries, for instance, the same problem exists, except that the competition comes from French books. So, in some of the smaller

39

countries, at least, there is a feeling of limitation, even of claustrophobia, among writers. I know Dutch writers and Dutch poets and critics who feel that their country is too small; and they think of a nation as being large, as America is large, and it gives them a sense of inferiority.

I cite these examples of others' problems to indicate that if American writers start to complain I think they're being a bit hasty. Their problems are so much less severe and their opportunities are so much greater than is the case in many countries. Even in a country like France, there are very, very few writers who can sustain themselves by writing, unless they happen to catch the American market. The same is true in England; the same is true in almost every country in the world.

Coming here on the plane, I read an article in a magazine called *Quest*, published in English in Bombay. The article was written by an Indian novelist and critic named Bay, and he talked of the problems of the Indian writer. He pointed out that, in a country bound by tradition and custom, as India is, with a caste system and social relationships that are, in general, very rigid; in a country that has now attained its independence and has also felt the impact of Western ideas, particularly from England; in a country that has a confident and perhaps rampant new nationalism—the national feeling of the first years of independence—the Hindu writer is faced with great dilemmas, and it is extremely difficult and perhaps impossible for him to communicate. He says that now it is felt, rightly or wrongly, that the writer must give expression to, must emphasize, must work on the principle that Indian values are superior to the cultural values of the West. He points out that this is a very disturbing problem for the Hindu novelist, and that it may overwhelm him.

All of these problems—the problem of a limited market, the fact that one might not be able to make a living as a writer and may have to write in one's spare time and take another form of work in order to gain one's bread, the danger of censorship from pressure groups, and so on—all of these problems are as nothing when compared with the situation of writers in totalitarian countries. We know enough about the condition and fate of writers in the Soviet Union to be sure of this. There is something shameful and disgusting in the endless spectacle of writers having to humiliate themselves, having to confess that they misunderstood the Party line. This has been going on decade after decade. It has been going on roughly since the second half of the 1920's. We know of cases of Russian writers of international stature, and in one case of greatness, who are among the disappeared and who either died in concentration camps or were killed. For instance, there is the writer I think of who was indubitably a great writer, Isaac Babel, author of two books of short stories that have been published in this country, one of them entitled *Red Cavalry*. Babal was, perhaps, the finest Russian short-story writer since Chekhov, and his name has not appeared in a dictionary or an encyclopedia of Soviet literature since about 1937. At one time he was recognized and hailed for his true greatness. Either he died in a concentration camp or he was murdered in one by the Russian secret police.

At the present time there are signs of what is called a "new awakening" in Russia, and there are official orders to writers that they may be freer and more critical; and we can see clearly that it will not be long before some Russian writer will be given the medal in the order of Stalin for writing the most severe, brutal and ruthless book about Stalin during the fourth Moscow trial. That is the trial of the ghost of Joseph Stalin. I state this because I want to emphasize that our experience—I don't mean our personal experience; I mean our historical experience of the rise of totalitarianism—has given new significance and new preciousness to the value of freedom. Writers were not free under Mussolini, and writers were not free in the time of Chekhov. In passing, I might mention a very humorous anecdote about literature under Mussolini. In Mussolini's last days, there was a translation of *Spoon River Anthology* by Edgar Lee Masters, who has a big reputation in Italy. The censors banned it, it was not allowed; so the translation was resubmitted and was called *S. Spoon River Anthology*. The censors then thought it was a book about a saint and let it be published.

Now, it may have been different in the past. In medieval society, for instance, there was great art produced in a society that was not democratic. But in our time, with the growth of science and the changing character of literature, it is very clear, it is patent, and I do not think it needs to be proved, that literature must be free. For literature to be free means that we must accept the principle that the writer has sovereignty over his own material and his own experience. All efforts to prevent or to destroy that sovereignty are an incursion upon freedom of expression.

Censorship, or the limitation of the sovereignty of the artist over his own experience, is an injury not solely to the writer; it's an injury to the reading public, too. We can now see with much greater clarity that bound up with freedom of expression should be freedom of access to information, including freedom of access to art and to literature. The conditions of development of national culture imply most clearly that each and all should have the opportunity to pick and choose what will be most meaningful, and most enjoyable, and most instructive to them.

There is a kind of cheap, trashy literature that is inevitable. It is produced and a quick penny is made from it. But it is separate from literature; it is separate from the serious rendition of human experience. What censors constantly do is to link the two together in an amalgam and then attempt to repress books that have been written with the aim of giving a thoughtful and true—true as the author sees and feels, at any rate—rendition of some feature of—if I may repeat a phrase that is perhaps too commonplace—our common human experience.

These are some aspects of writing, and this is the substance of what I wished to say in this lecture.

Q.: What occupation would you consider best suited to supplying breadth to the writer?

A.: Well, how do I know? Those are questions that are concrete and specific. It's meaningless to give general answers to them.

Q.: I was thinking of a remark of Mr. Ginsberg's that impressed me. He suggested we go out and dig ditches rather than associating with journalists or teaching. I wonder if you hold that view.

A.: I don't hold any view on it. I would say this: that it's an individual problem and it's also a question of opportunity. I'm sure that Mr. Ginsberg, who is unquestionably an estimable man and a good and honest publisher, would rather remain a publisher than decide to be a writer and then go out and dig ditches himself. But I do think that it's an individual matter, depending upon what is easiest for the writer to write, how much money he needs and what jobs he can get. Right now you can get lots of jobs. There was a time when you couldn't get any jobs. By the way, Dreiser once worked as a laborer, but not for long. He also worked as an editor of a magazine and made ten thousand dollars a year, in 1907, which was not inconsiderable.

Q.:...Supposing there could be a change in the manner or style of writing, away from the realistic. What do you suppose it might be?

A.: That's a question that is so hypothetical I don't know what to say. There have been changes. There are a number of contemporary books that don't fit what we call the realistic style; and there are a great number of critics who attack realism and claim that realistic writers are not writers, that they're old-fashioned, that they ought to do something else. One common notion today is that a book cannot be a great book unless it's what is called an allegory. For instance, there has been a critical study written about the symbolism of Ernest Hemingway by a certain most erudite professor at Princeton. And thinking back to the 1920's and thinking of the characters in Ernest Hemingway's books, I'm certain that if Hemingway had read this study he must have consumed about a gallon of Scotch or had high blood pressure or had a stroke. He'd think it was nonsense. Then we have the case of Franz Kafka. I spoke at a symposium at Rochester University, where another very erudite professor and teacher, Dr. Mark Shorer—I believe he's at the University of California or Southern California—gave a paper. In it, he set down a rigid set of prescriptions or rules defining what a novel was. And it ended by the exclusion of Dickens and Fielding and almost every novel that we've read and loved for generations. If I might be personal, afterward I made the remark that somehow or other this reminded me of Woodrow Wilson, who, when he was president of Princeton University and was undergoing a struggle with the trustees, was supposed to have said to newspaper men in Pittsburgh: "How can I have democracy at Princeton University when they won't do what I tell them?" I said that I had been reading and writing books for over twenty-five years and that I was bewildered, that I didn't know what the hell Professor Shorer was talking about. I didn't think that *he* did. It is a matter of how I can write books or read books when I won't do what Professor Shorer wants done; and I really don't think he knows what he means when he says what he wants.

I am against the whole business of telling writers that they've got to belong to this or that tradition. You have to find your own temperament and write out of it. I believe that the best condition is one in which there is free play of tendencies and each writes and reads that which is profitable and meaningful to him. I don't think that there is any kind of meaning to be had from thinking that there will be a victory of one tendency over another. If books that are called realistic are disturbing or troublesome to you, read something else. If you feel that you cannot or do not want to write them—that you do not have the kind of insights and interests to see the way most realistic writers do—but you see in another way, write in that way. What is important about writing is its richness and variety.

I would add this. Think about yourself in the course of a day. You like many contradictory things. You like some ordinary or commonplace things. There's a whole variety of likes and dislikes, including likes and dislikes of phrases heard and expressed and of objects in the physical world seen. We not only welcome but *have* a kind of primitive or elemental variety in our personal, day-by-day life, and in the same way I think we should welcome that kind of variety in literature and in all other forms of art.

Q.: Well, maybe the writer had in mind the significance of that statement you made about heightened consciousness. Would that indicate a change of style or a different emphasis in that respect?

A.: There *are* changes of style and trend. Each generation is different from the previous generation and writes differently. That happens. There's a dual character about what we see and think. On the one hand there's a common element, because there are common elements in our environment. On the other hand there's an individual and a singular element. The differentiation among people is something that is so amazing we never realize it. There's an extraordinary book called *Truants from Life*, by Dr. Bruno Bettelheim of the University of Chicago. He runs a school for psychotic children and has had remarkable results. This book consists of four case histories of children who were put into school in very bad shape. They were, in common language, crazy or insane. Dr. Bettelheim shows how they were helped. And one is amazed by the differences in these four sick children. There, in the extreme case, you see how much originality, individuality, there is in human beings. And that is quite so in writers. Writers quite frequently are original and obstreperous people who are, in many instances, at war with their environment, and their individuality sometimes becomes emphasized, or overemphasized. I think that there is no need to worry that there will not be changes of trend, but I do not think that they should be artificially created. In most cases, I do not think that one can say, "This kind of thing has been done, so I'm going to create something new."

Q.: This is a personal question, and if you don't want to answer I should be happy just the same. Is it easier now to be Mr. Farrell than it was twenty or thirty years ago?

A.: Well, I want to assure your happiness, because I think we all should be happy. I would say that sometimes it's easier and sometimes it's harder. Today it was easier and yesterday it was hard as the devil. Any more questions?

Q.: I'd like to ask a question and have my curiosity settled. What are you doing here when the White Sox are opening today? But seriously—you're one of the few writers with an established reputation both as a fiction writer and as a critic. Do you find that a good grouping?

A.: Well, I'm sorry that I'm here instead of in Chicago. I was supposed to have gone to Chicago and I wanted to write about the White Sox opening, but instead I talked about the problems of writing. Whether it's fortunate or unfortunate, even a writer must make a living and support his family. And, secondly—I don't know whether it's fortunate or unfortunate, but it's the way I am—some writers function both as critics, or as alleged critics, and as novelists; and some don't. I just happen to; and perhaps it's a temperamental weakness, never to allow myself to sit still in one place or sit still with one profession or one set of ideas. That's the way I am and maybe it's good or maybe it's bad, maybe it's fortunate or maybe it's unfortunate, but I'm not too dissatisfied with it.

Q.: . . . about censors and criteria for defining censorable books?

A.: Of course, the thing we can *do* about censors, we can beat them. Don't forget that. We frequently do. But I would say this: that it's much easier to know a good or serious book than to define it. Secondly, I do not think that it is my problem to produce a law. There are many laws on the books and I think that our legislators should be capable of framing a law and that our judges should be capable—and our judges in many instances are.

"I believe there are more people who want to write books than who want to play baseball—and this is a nation of frustrated baseball writers . . ."

Questions and Answers

At the University of Kentucky, February 18, 1955

Part of the democratic way of life is the chance and the opportunity and the desire to grow and to develop. I've used the word culture many times, and I would say this. The culture of a time or a period is a reflection, a revelation, a concentrated picturing or expression of the way men and women of that time thought and felt about themselves, about their past and their future and about the work they did, individually and collectively. I think that with the freedom we have had and have, and with the wealth, the educational opportunities, the means of communication, we have now within our hands—within our means—the chance to create, to produce, an astonishing cultural renaissance in this country. Everything is waiting in America now for a tremendously new and vitally significant expression or revelation of the spirit of man—or the spirit of man as he has developed on our continent and in our country. That is, in substance, what I think about life in the United States.

Moderator: Mr. Farrell knows a great number of answers to a great number of questions, and he has consented to answer what questions you have from the floor. If you'll rise and wave your hand and state your question, why, Mr. Farrell will answer it.

Farrell: I don't know if I know so many answers, but I'll try to say something.

Q.: You said we have an opportunity for a mass culture. Would you say that America is actually heading in the direction of a genuine mass culture . . . as the trend of TV and other mass instruments of communication comes into being? Is it actually heading in that direction or does it simply have the opportunity and the possibility to do so?

A.: I would say that there are many things to indicate that we don't have a genuine mass culture, that it's being thwarted. Many of the productions on TV are very bad. When I say very bad, I don't want to imply that this is a question of taste. I would say that they are counterfeit, they're insincere. I would say another indication is many of the comic books. But at the same time that this has happened, we've had an increase in reading, and an increase in reading of significant books. We've had both tendencies at work at the same time. Now we can't

46

think of everybody liking—let us take any selective figure—say, Bach or Beethoven. We shouldn't think of culture in those terms. We should think of it in terms of accessibility to like or dislike what one chooses. I cannot gauge tendencies, but I can say, and I repeat, that there is a danger in this country of creating the robot consumer; there is a danger of passivity. I might even go further and say that it might well develop in the future that the world will be divided into those who read and those who don't read; and those who don't read will be passive and told what to do, and those who read will have the important positions and influence in society. That is a possibility. But not all the signs have been of cultural decline in the United States. The response to writing, the audience for literature, is much greater than it was twenty or thirty years ago. Twenty or thirty years ago, a writer of corresponding position to mine wouldn't have had as many people come to hear him talk at a university. At the University of Chicago, Sherwood Anderson would have been lucky to have had an audience this large. So there has been an increase of interest, too. This is an empirical question. We can't absolutely answer it. I will state flatly that there are dangerous tendencies, and by dangerous tendencies I mean tendencies that create a sense of phoniness and counterfeit; but I can't give a positive answer either way. I would state that universities have become tremendously important now. In the 1920's it was standard to laugh at college professors; H. L. Mencken used to berate them, etc. But the situation has changed. The universities are becoming significant repositories of American and world culture in the United States. And, particularly in the universities, the effort must be made to create an interest in and enthusiasm for literature and ideas. However, literature and ideas are important only if they have some meaning, if they help you to see and feel life more deeply, to make you more aware; if a person does not go to them in this way, it is just as well that he looks at TV. That isn't a decisive answer to your question, but it's about the best I can say. There is a possibility of a development in either direction.

Q.: Don't you think we ought to put more stress on education—the means for disseminating these ideas? Take a radio for instance—it's been with us a good while and a mere twist of the knob will turn on highbrow or lowbrow music, but the supply and demand has been such that there are very few classical programs on the radio anymore. Don't you think that supply and demand have something to do with it and that, if we had more education, these would cling together?

A.: I don't know either way. Of course, I don't look at culture only in the sense of, say, classical music. I think that the United States, in

47

producing jazz, is producing something that is significant and quite important, a new and distinctive aspect of American culture. I don't see why a person can't listen to both Bach and jazz music. I think it's also possible that out of television we may create a new art. I haven't seen this but I was told about it yesterday . . . A story was put on television of the murder of Leon Trotsky, and according to the account as it was given to me, it was a true account of the facts and it was apparently a good dramatization. I've seen some of the television in France and they have many good plays on. And there are more good things on American television than we realize, although there is this cheap, canned stuff. There is a need on the part of many people for escape. And I don't have, *ipso facto*, any objection to escape movies and escape books. I don't have, *ipso facto*, any objection to who-done-its. I object only when there is a confusion of values—when we begin to take hokum for something that it isn't, when we confuse hokum with the sincere expression and revelation of human feelings and experience. And that brings me to the point that there is a need for much greater criticism. Our critics have let us down very badly, particularly the "new critics," who make of literature a kind of a scholastic rite, and who contrive all sorts of symbolic meanings of books and with them deaden our feeling for the books themselves. They deaden the response; they write for one another. I think that if we had a more vital and vigorous criticism, we would have a healthier literary situation. Now, we're talking about some very broad things. We're talking of things about which we can't be very conclusive here. Generally speaking, it is a fact about the United States that it's so big that anything you say about it is true and the opposite is true. There has always been a tendency toward cheapness and vulgarization, and there has been a developing serious American culture in our own time, too, and most certainly in American literature. American literature has perhaps become the outstanding literature in the world today, although it will take the Europeans twenty or thirty more years to realize it.

Q.: Mr. Farrell, you mentioned that there is something significant in the reawakening of the spirit of man in this country. Do you feel that that is a lag in our literature or that it's merely a point of time until this will evolve here?

A.: I don't know. That is, I can't say, because I can't predict the future. Broadly, I would say that in the twentieth century there has developed a genuine literature in this country, which deals with the life and feeling of people here and now, which deals with a significant rendering of characters and events in the America of our time. Characters like Lewis's Babbitt have been created in our literature. Will this continue in the future? I don't know. You cannot predict where and when talent will arise. You can only attempt to preserve a cultural continuity and to create those conditions wherein if talent does arise, it will find its own voice and a way to some kind of a successful expression and development. I won't predict that there will or there won't. I will say again that it is possible that there can be a great cultural renaissance in this country. It's possible, but I won't go further than that. I will also grant that it's possible that there will be a deadening, a soddening of feeling through cultural imitations. And I would say that the question has been posed whether sincerity or the counterfeit will, in the long run, win out.

Q.: Mr. Farrell, I wonder if you could look at . . . this question from, perhaps, another angle and tell us what things of value you think radio and television are now contributing toward society?

A.: Very little. I would say this . . . in TV, one of the main ones I've seen was the political reporting . . . the reporting of events is very good. And occasionally comedians like George Gobel and Jackie Gleason are good. Now, I don't see too much TV—and I was out of the country for six months, and so I got further behind—but I did see, for instance, a wonderful French pantomime on television. Most of the movies I've seen have been pretty commonplace. I'm told—I haven't seen them, but I'm told—that some of the United States Steel ones, *Omnibus*, are better. On the whole, I'd say that there is more produced that is banal, unserious and cheap, and I think the same is true in radio. There is this question: whether or not it will be different in literature. There are more cheap books produced than good books; but the good books survive and the cheap books are forgotten. I don't know whether that will happen in television. I would say that television has had a beneficial effect on the motion pictures, which have been getting much better. For instance, ten years ago *On the Waterfront* would have been impossible; and several other significant motion pictures have been produced since television became a menace to the industry. There was a very good production of Stephen Crane's *Red Badge of Courage*. *Sister Carrie* and a new version of *An American Tragedy* were produced, and they were honest, good pictures. I've seen some terribly bad and silly stuff on television, but I think it is possible by criticism to contribute toward improving it. I don't think we are always necessarily going to get the same kind of stale, insincere, counterfeit rendition of human feelings we get from TV now. I think it is possible to change that—through criticism and analysis, and particularly through education in the colleges. Universities should offer courses in television. Studies should be made of what

49

happens and how we feel when we look at it. When we begin to acquire a body of knowledge we can develop a criticism so that the next generation that goes into this field will be better prepared to make a fight inside these arts to improve them.

Q.: Mr. Farrell, I would like to ask you what you think of Thomas Wolfe as an American writer.

A.: Well, I'll tell you—what I say about Thomas Wolfe will be based upon my memory of having read him, and I haven't read Thomas Wolfe for, oh, at least twenty years. At the time I felt that there was an emotional thinness and a kind of perpetual adolescence in Thomas Wolfe, and at the same time tremendous energy and verve and spirit. I think that he was quite wonderful and often poetic in rendering atmospheres, in rendering sights and sounds. I think that the emotional patterns in his work are monotonous—a young man is always pitted against a world that never understands him. There is an inequality in the sympathy that he gives to Eugene Gant, or other representations of himself, and that he gives to everyone else. That is what I meant by emotional monotony and adolescent character. I think he was tremendously gifted. There were temperamental differences between him and me—I at least like to think that I am more analytical, and that, perhaps, gave me a certain antipathy to his work. I intend to reread it. But I would say this—that, to me, the most valuable feature of his work is his wonderful ability to render the qualities of an atmosphere. He was more responsive to those, I believe, than he was to people. I think that he had much to learn about human emotions and that it is a great tragedy that he died, because, most certainly, a man such as he might well have developed a great deal.

Q.: Mr. Farrell, do you think there is any danger of our contemporary forms of culture exerting a bad moral influence today?

A.: Well, now, what do you mean by a bad moral influence?

Q.: I mean, we have such an excess of violence in our literature and in television. Do you think that that can possibly have a bad moral effect?

A.: Do I think what will have a bad moral effect?

Q.: These productions and these books, and——

A.: You see, there are several things. I'm really not sure what is on your mind. I wonder if what you're getting at is: Do I think that realistic writings or a frank treatment of amorous experience will demoralize youth, and there should be censorship? Is that what you are driving at, or not?

Q.: I have more in mind—violence, murder . . .

A.: Well, how much of a bad moral effect that will have I don't know, but I don't think that it is good. I've noticed something: In many motion pictures, there not only has to be a fight, there has to be a very sadistic and brutal fight. Right after the war there was a stupid and inexcusable sadism in many motion pictures. And I notice in many comic strips that every word the characters say to one another is an insult and sort of denigrates human beings. I don't think that this can have a good moral effect, but what are you going to do about it? I don't think that you should censor it. I think that, in the last analysis, people just have to grow up or not grow up. It is really very hard to speak strictly and say what is the moral influence of any kind of work on a person. By and large, I think that TV and comics and radio and everything have less influence on children than do fathers and mothers and teachers. The example in the home is much more important than all of these things put together. But further, what you ask is really a factual question that would have to be examined factually. All I can give is an answer based on impressions and speculations. I would like to see some serious empirical investigation of these questions, questions relating to the moral affect of art and the relationship of these things to delinquency, and so on. A whole team would have to carry such an investigation out. I think we would get some insight into the nature of our society. And I think also if that, if it were made, many of the demands and claims of the censors could then be factually refuted.

Q.: Mr. Farrell, I suppose the problem of thoughtful authors getting access to an audience has always been a basic one, but Malcolm Cowley, the *Saturday Review* and others seem to be more concerned about it today than ever—talking about publishers being unwilling to take anything. . .

A.: First of all, let me say that there is a need for serious literature in a society, but there is no necessary need for a particular writer. When a new writer starts to write and publish, there is no need for him and there is no market for his work. That has to be created—through making his work accessible and also through critics and others. Secondly, I would say that it *is* more difficult now than it was in the past, because there is a crisis in the book business. The trade books are too highly priced, and there has been much competition among the reprint houses, and, of course, with that, some fly-by-night publishers have come upon the scene and filled the stands with stuff like *Lillie of Paris*, *Sins of Paris* and *Sweets of Paris*, and it's all junk. There has been further competition there. In the same way there is a crisis practically all over the world. There's a world-wide crisis in the book business. Perhaps the one exception is Germany. In other countries it's worse. Someone told me that Malcolm Cowley said that in the United

States about two hundred writers can live from their writing. Well, the same proportion can't be said to live from writing in other countries. But then there is a second question. Are there two hundred writers in America who have something worth saying? There will always be a lot of writing and just a little that's worth reading. There will always be more books—there will always be more writers—than there are readers for them. It's an inevitable situation. I believe there are more people who want to write books than who want to play baseball, and this is a nation of frustrated baseball players. It's doubly a nation of frustrated writers. One person has calculated that there are something like 16,360,000 people who want to write. So it's always going to be an overcrowded field. But at the present time it is worse than it was in other years, and there is likely to be less inclination on the part of publishers to take chances. It's worse even for poets, and the basic reason is prices. The price of books is too high, and the costs of production are such that the publishers can't bring it down. So we're in a crisis. There is the same situation in England. In France it is so bad that publishers often don't want to publish books and look for subsidies. I don't think there is a healthy and promising situation for young writers at the present time. In recent years, there has been. It's a striking thing—think of the number of writers who from 1933 to the present have become established with one book. William Saroyan, Richard Wright, Truman Capote, a whole series of writers. For years, the situation was very good for young writers. Now, because of prices it's threatening to change. Another thing is that fiction is selling less than it usd to—particularly original trade-fiction books, which are selling very badly. I think that the book business will survive. I think that, in time, something else will happen—TV will limit, if not totally destroy, the market for certain kinds of adventure books and so on, and that it will drive out a certain number of bad books. If so, that will be to the good. More questions?

Q.: Mr. Farrell, I believe you stated a few minutes ago, in answer to a question, that you didn't think movies, and books, and things like that had any such determining influence as the household does on a child. Does this mean that you think that sparing the rod will spoil the child and be a definite cause of juvenile delinquency?

A.: Let me think a moment first. I might have overstated. But then— sparing the rod and spoiling the child—I wasn't advocating that you beat your children up. I would say that, basically, if a child is in a home where there is love and where there are responsible parents, the likelihood of his becoming a delinquent is very small. And I think that more important than seeing something in a motion picture is the faith in human beings and the faith in love or the lack of thereof that comes mainly from the home situation. That is what I had in mind. Now, the question of juvenile delinquency is a very complicated one; the country is full of committees talking about it and studying it, and I won't attempt to make statements and judgments about it here. I'm not sure about a number of the questions involved. I am sure about this: Serious books do not make prostitutes and juvenile delinquents. I don't think that *An American Tragedy* is going to make a juvenile delinquent. I don't think that *Madame Bovary* is going to produce a prostitute. And I will assert this with conviction: When serious books are attacked as the cause of social evils of this kind, it is mendacious nonsense. Certain kinds of sadistic motion pictures and sadistic comic books—I don't know, but they possibly may have some contributory effect. I'd like to see more investigation of the question. But even if you grant that, I would insist that love and responsibility—the attitude and situation in the home—are the basic factors. I think they are the basic factor.

Realism in Literature

Speech delivered at Rutgers University, April 6, 1956

You know, I have thought about how I would discuss this question tonight. I have made various notes, considered various approaches and then decided that I would try to be as simple as I absolutely could. An anecdote occurs to me, something that happened in Chicago recently. A friend of mine runs a school for disturbed children. His name is Dr. Bruno Bettelheim. He has written a book that is a classic in its field. The book is called *Love Is Not Enough*. A child was brought to him. This child had a reading problem; the child was also psychotic. In examining the child, the following was revealed: In the textbooks that were given to this disturbed little boy, there were stories about how mommy loves poppy, how poppy loves mommy, how brothers and sisters love each other. This child lived in a home where people were tearing themselves apart with hatred. When the little boy was given a reader, he found these exercises that told of a false love, a love that wasn't true for this boy—and he resisted them to the point where he would not read. I mention that for this reason. Is or is not the truth of significance in our lives? Should we feed ourselves with illusions or should we attempt to look at reality and to see it as clearly, as nakedly, as we can?

A second anecdote occurs to me: Maxim Gorky tells a story about Leo Tolstoy. Tolstoy was an old man when Gorky met him. Gorky told him that he had seen an old woman with a little boy. The old woman was the grandmother of the boy. The old woman was drunk; she was drunk to the point where he could not control her bladder, and she was urinating in the gutter, and this frightened little boy, her grandson, was looking on. It was a horrible incident as Gorky saw it, and as Tolstoy saw it, too. Tolstoy said to him, "Don't write that. Never write it." Then Tolstoy thought for a moment, and he said, "No, you must write it. You must tell all. If you don't, the eyes of that little boy will haunt you."

Now, these two anecdotes tell the whole story of realism in literature. They tell the story of whether we should feed ourselves with illusions or should attempt to look directly, and if necessary, nakedly at life. The first one reveals this: that if we do not attempt to tell the truth, to see life as it is; if we do not attempt to look at ourselves, to look at others, to look at human nature as it is, what will happen? Will a new generation of children feel that they have been lied to and become bitter to the point of showing great resistance? Second—how will we feel if we do not tell the truth, if we do not at least attempt to tell the truth? Will we be haunted? In other words, what the psychoanalyst calls the reality principle and, secondly, our own guilt, our own conscience—these are the reasons we should attempt to see life realistically. And if we attempt to see life realistically, we should write about it that way.

The simplest definition of realism in literature is this: that experience is grounded in reality and that there is no other source of experience but the world we know; that there is no supernatural sanction and no supernatural cause; that there is no extra-experiential basis for experience. In other words, what happens happens in this world; it is explainable in this world.

For a number of decades now, writers have attempted to come to terms with worldly experience. The great Russian writers—Tolstoy, Dostoyevsky, Turgenev, Chekov—the great tradition in French literature from Balzac and Stendahl to Marcel Proust, English writers such as Thomas Hardy and American writers from Stephen Crane and Harold Frederic, the author of *The Damnation of Theron Ware*, and Theodore Dreiser to the present have attempted to come to some kind of terms with life as we live it. And almost every generation of writers that has attempted to see human experience straight and clear has solicited the attention of the police. There have been censorship trials, the academies have attacked them, the ministers and the priests have attacked them; the Philistines, the comfortable middle class, the businessmen have attacked them. So I propose on the basis of this to ask a simple question: Is the truth worth knowing?

American literature in the nineteenth century, with the exception of Walt Whitman, Mark Twain, Melville and Hawthorne, was a literature that was colonial in character and that was based upon a series of illusions. It was based upon Victorian illusions about human nature. At the end of the nineteenth century we had a change in American writing; we had the growth of realism.

Before I go on with that, I want to make a few remarks. In Europe, particularly in France and Russia, the literature was a literature in which life was seen with greater clarity than it was in the Victorian age in England or in nineteenth-century America. A novel occurs to me, a novel that is not read much in America. It is one of the books that has influenced the whole history of literature, particularly in France. The book is called *Le Liasons Dangereuses*. A recent translation of it has occurred under the title *Dangerous Acquaintances*. The author was named Pierre Choderlos de la Clos. La Clos was a general in the army of Louis XVI and was a noble courtier. The book was written in the 1780's, just prior to the French Revolution. It is the story of a series of love affairs, or a series of *liasons*. There are two extremely evil characters in it, a French nobleman and a woman, Madame de Merteuil. They both attempt to rule and to destroy other people. There is a young girl who is completely destroyed. There is a married woman, a virtuous woman, who is destroyed by the chief protagonist. La Clos was himself a general, and he describes this series of love affairs in terms of strategy. The book was attacked as a book that cast a very bad light on life among the nobility in the old regime in France. La Clos was ruined and his career in the French Army was ended because of this book. The middle-class people, who were against the old regime, hailed it.

Now, was it worthwhile for La Clos to tell the truth? Should he have risked his career, his future? Or should he not have told the truth? This is a problem that every serious writer of every generation faces. Should he or should he not come to terms with reality?

I come back to my definition of realism as an attempt to deal with life as it is, as one sees it. And I come back to what I said about American literature. In the nineteenth century we had, in the main, a colonial literature that attempted to show life in a false light. It avoided dealing with the facts of amorous relationships and avoided dealing with the facts of misery. At the end of the nineteenth century we had a series of writers. One of them was Harold Frederic, another was Henry James, another was Stephen Crane. Stephen Crane wrote a novel called *Maggie, A Girl of the Streets*. *Maggie* was a prophetic book. It is the story of a prostitute living on the east side of New York, the story of a girl who is ruined. The dialogue is in the vernacular. The spelling is phonetic. The book shows a class of people and a kind of a life that was different from the accepted, conventional upper-class life of the period. We see that there is another life. It is a life of people who are restricted; who have had no education and have not had contact with and have not participated in any significant way in the culture of their times. *Maggie* was written when Stephen Crane was twenty-one or twenty-two. It was a prophetic work because it predicted the future of American literature.

The second writer I mentioned, Harold Frederic, wrote *The Damnation of Theron Ware*. Theron Ware was a minister living in a small upstate New York town. This was a backward town, in the sense that we would consider it uncivilized, or relatively uncivilized. It was parochial. Theron Ware meets three people. He meets a Catholic priest who is representative not of Irish Catholicism but of continental Catholicism, and who is sophisticated, intelligent and has a kind of Jesuitical attitude about the people; a girl who represents the attitude of the *fin de siècle*, the decade of Oscar Wilde and Aubrey Beardsley; and a doctor who has been influenced by Darwinian science. Now, these three people represent attitudes toward life and a certain cultivation that Theron Ware has never met with before. They represent three European attitudes—nineteenth-century continental religion, nineteenth-century art and nineteenth-century science. Theron Ware attempts to live with and by the attitudes of these three people and he cannot do it. He is not prepared for it. As a consequence, he destroys himself—he becomes a moral wreck. The damnation of Theron Ware is that he cannot achieve a higher individuality by assimilating sophisticated European attitudes.

Books like *Maggie* and *The Damnation of Theron Ware* were the beginning of an attempt to see American life as it is.

In 1919, H. L. Mencken wrote an essay on American literature, and in it he said that the average hero in American writing (as of that time, I add) was a third-rate man. He was possibly an advertising agent or a public-relations man. He met the daughter of a hook-and-eye-factory magnate, he gobbled up the hook-and-eye factory and married the daughter and was a success. Mencken remarked that the difference between such characters and the characters of great literature is that many of the great books or fundamental works deal with a person who is more sensitive than that; who does not desire merely to gobble up a hook-and-eye factory but desires to come to terms with his own destiny—and nine times out of ten, when a man comes to terms with the fiats of destiny, he fails. And that, Mencken tells us, is the reason why a number of the great novels of all time were novels of decay, novels in which a man attempts to meet his fate and fails.

Now, there is a kind of false optimism in our life in America. There is an optimism that is based upon the notion that anything is possible and everything is simple. A number of the great novels—Dostoyevsky's *Crime and Punishment* and *The Brothers Karamazov*, Tolstoy's *Anna Karenina*, Flaubert's *Madame Bovary*, to name a few—are books that emphasize or reveal, by a concrete story, the fact that life is *not* simple. But there has been in the American educational system, and in our culture, a Victorian influence that would make life simpler than it is and that is resistant to a literature that would deal with people in what seem to be the real ways in which human destinies unfold. . . .

So, realism in literature, and particularly in American literature, has developed in opposition to simplified attitudes about virtue and sin, about black and white and human conduct inherited from the Victorians. It has evolved in revolt against a series of conventional images of life as well. American realism has been a literature of rebellion for the simple reason that the effort to describe characters and events in the way in which an author saw them was so resisted. There were so many efforts to censor it. The suppression of *Sister Carrie* in 1900 almost epitomizes the struggle of the American writer. Other significant American writers were neglected and scorned. Walt Whitman died in neglect—he was considered an immoral fellow. His experiences were more frustrating than Dreiser's. And to this day, if we look at our slick magazines, if we consider the great majority of movie plots and television stories, we can recognize that still there is this effort to simplify life, this seeing of people as either all good or all bad, this presentation of life in terms of cheap, easy and banally optimistic stories.

Is it important to attempt to take a clearer and more realistic measure of life, or should we fill ourselves and others with these simple and childish dreams? Is it significant that, in one way or another, a great deal of our literature, a great deal of our culture, is an elaboration of that simple story of mommy loving poppy and poppy loving mommy that caused Dr. Bettelheim's boy to refuse to read? Or is it important that we destroy such stereotypes and attempt to see life in a more complicated way?

Part of the answer to these questions can be found in the story of the American melting pot. It is the story of new types, new groups— economically, nationally and racially—giving expression to a common American life. You know, if you looked at the football roster of Notre Dame thirty or forty years ago, nearly all the names were Irish; now there are Poles, there are Bohemians, there as Slavs and there are Italians. And it is the same way in the story of American literature. In our popular writing of fifty years ago, we had the stage Irishman, the stage Negro, the stage Jew, the stage servant; in other words, those who were considered socially or racially inferior were treated comically. Today there has been a tearing down of this notion of Nordic superiority. If you consider the backgrounds of some of the writers and characters of the last twenty to thirty years, you will see it. You have Erskine Caldwell dealing with the poor Southern farmer. You have Richard Wright dealing with Negroes in Chicago. You have Claude McKay describing a Pullman porter in his novel *Home to Harlem*. I could give a whole series like this—of people with backgrounds that were heretofore considered inferior now represented in our literature.

So, particularly in the last twenty years, we have had a literature that deals with what we will call a common life—the streets, the pool rooms, the poor farms, the Negro. It's a literature that deals with these types and these aspects of American experience more realistically than had been done before. Types that had been treated comically or as commonplace now are treated as characters who have a certain importance, a certain human dignity. An attempt to deal with the worth of experience of those groups that have been scorned, or considered inferior groups, both in our social attitudes and in our literature, has become an important aspect of realism, and this must be taken into consideration when we talk about it.

There is a difference in the European realistic novel. Most of the European novels of the nineteenth century deal with superior young men—with the evolution of the superior young man in his struggle with his destiny. Balzac's novel, *Lost Illusions*, is the story of a young man coming to Paris full of illusions and then losing them and becoming corrupted. Stendahl's *The Red and the Black* and Flaubert's finest novel, *A Sentimental Education,* are stories of gifted young men coming to the city and struggling against society. In American literature, on the whole, most of the heroes, most of the chief protagonists, have been representative of what we call the average man. American literature most definitely, most clearly emphasizes that one point. I mean it deals with the experience of the ordinary person; in this there is a special character to American literature. And that special character is this: It is a literature attempting honestly and frankly to tell the story of the average man.

Now, I mentioned earlier that there has been a whole series of attacks on realistic writing. I'd like to make this point more clearly, and to show that there is a certain snobbery at work here, by telling of a personal experience. About seven years ago there were assaults on books in Philadelphia. One Saturday afternoon, the police went around with vans and they seized books, including a number of my books. As a consequence of these seizures, we sued the police—went into court and sued them for damages. There were two cases. One was in the state courts of Pennsylvania in Philadelphia, which we won, and the second was in the Federal courts. In our case in the Federal courts, there was a minister who would come and talk to me every day after I testified. On the first day he said that he had prayed for me and that he wanted me to read certain passages of Saint Paul. I replied that he had caused me sufficient trouble and I didn't want to talk to him. On the second day, I changed my tactics. I said, "You know, you're a bad boy. You're not only doing damage to me, you're doing damage to the Constitution. You shouldn't do this. You shouldn't act this way.

You know you don't believe it." Well, after three days of court hearings he came up to me and he said, "You know, Mr. Farrell, I think you're a genius and I wouldn't object to your books being read except that they're sold at twenty-five and thirty-five cents and the wrong kind of people will read them." I think that a great deal of the objection to realism is simply this—that the wrong kind of people will read it. In other words, that the great majority of people in this country will have access to culture and they will be able to read, to select works that attempt to reflect life in clearer terms than those that are presented in the false oversimplifications of cheap popular fiction and of cheap movies.

Now let me just repeat that realism only means an attempt to present seriously, honestly and frankly images of life as it is. When I say "images of life as it is" I must add: as a particular writer sees them. Writers see life differently. All of us see characters and events differently. What is important in art is that a writer struggle to attain, express and reveal his own vision of experience. All this means is that in realism the writer, the artist, the novelist attempts to see life clearly and plausibly, instead of in terms of illusions.

The title of my lecture is "Realism—What Is It, and What's Wrong with It?" About the second coordinate clause—there is nothing wrong with it unless we make this statement: It is wrong to attempt to see people as they are rather than in terms of moral and optimistic illusions about them. I answer the question, then, by saying that there is nothing wrong with it. I think that we *should* attempt to see people as they are rather than by means of easy, cheap, suave illusions and stereotypes, such as those that are given to us in motion pictures and newspaper editorials and the like.

I would like to repeat once more that there is a special character to American realism. This special character is that it deals with the American melting pot; it deals with the ordinary person to a degree that we do not find in realistic writings in Europe. The average American, the ordinary person, has become the hero or chief protagonist of American literature. At one time, this was very disturbing to a number of professors who wanted to be able to apply the Aristotelian conception of tragedy to novels, and who assumed that to be a tragic hero one had to be superior, had to be more aware. But we live in a kind of society and in a kind of world where there is no opportunity for people to be superior in the Aristotelian sense. That is given only to a few. We live in a society where the average person struggles to achieve significance, meaning and value in his own life. The realistic American novel is a representation of that struggle, and it is a representation of the cost of what American development means. I think it has been most important. I think that it dramatizes the story of values in this country. Many of our realistic books are very critical of values, but I think that is important, too. And I think it is of the greatest importance that a man like Dreiser could cast a sharp, clear and critical reflection of American values on the culture at large.

I'd like to make one final point. When we talk of realism, we don't talk only of its treatment of life as it is but also of the reflection it casts on values. Realistic writing shows the way people attempt to live by one or another set of values. And I think that it is important to remember that. With these remarks in mind, I repeat: Realism in literature is an attempt to deal with life as it is, in all its complexity. There is nothing wrong with that, not if we are going to locate ourselves in the universe, to see where we are, to attempt to have a clearer, franker and more honest viewpoint toward life. It is important that both in our thinking and in our literature we all attempt to see life realistically. I think that most of the attacks upon realistic writing are fraudulent; they are hypocritical, they are unfair and they are snobbish. Because again I emphasize, and I close with this remark: Realism in literature is an effort to see life clear, and true, and honestly.

The 1920's in American Life and Literature

Selected passages from a speech delivered at Duke
University, Durham, North Carolina, December 17, 1957

I said that I was going to speak about the 1920's. I was thinking about those years at dinner and was thinking about them back-stage—the years of the youth of some of us—and it occurred to me that the United States of America, at least in that department of its life governed by its intelligentsia, so-called, is forever growing up. Back in the 1920's it was said that America was coming of age; and I have been hearing this again and again, with each new genera-tion, all through my literary life. Now we have Leslie Fiedler com-ing of age by looking back at the 1920's. He is one of the represen-tatives of his generation—it's a generation of youth, but with a lit-tle bit of the alderman on its stomach and a little bit of gray in its hair; but they are still young writers—*Partisan Review* writers and the like. One of them is Leslie Fiedler, who has written a book called *The Age of Innocence,* which holds that all previous genera-tions of writers, prior to Leslie Fiedler, who has written one book and two or three short stories, were innocent. The new generation is no longer innocent; the great theme of American culture today is how, finally, America has come of age. Along with this theme come interpretations of past decades, especially the 1920's and 1930's, but these interpretations are usually a matter of cliches.

There's a habit in American literary journalism and editing of looking up each successive decade, of finding one or two aspects of conduct in it and presenting them as the defining characteristics of that period of American life; and then of assuming that, in the following ten years, everything changed. For about ten or twenty years the writers of one decade are attacked and forgotten and then they are restored; but they are usually restored by cliches, and there are many cliches and many stereotypes occurring at the present time. The generation that finally is no longer innocent is now making symbolic interpretations of some of the writers in the 1920's. They're finding Christ images and many other images and

62

symbols, and all this would have been foreign to the people of the 1920's, and it would have been foreign to the writers of that period.

Now, the 1920's are important in American life for more reasons than that it was the era of Prohibition and was called the Roaring Twenties. It is important for more reasons than that there were dramatic features of the life of the times. It marked a turning point in the history of America—politically, socially, culturally and economically. The United States became the chief producer of industrial goods in about 1883. After the First World War, in which the United States intervened late, America became a creditor rather than a debtor nation. Basic capital investment had been made and the industrial structure of the country was established. Those of you who are students have undoubtedly read of the prosperity of the twenties. It was a prosperity that has been surpassed by the postwar prosperity of the last twelve years; but before our own time, it was, perhaps, the most prosperous period in the history of America. Because it was so prosperous, it has come to be believed that the entire nation spent its time playing the stock market and watching Babe Ruth hit home runs, which is not quite true.

One of the defining differences we can see after the First World War is that we have the beginning then of what is now quite a clear and apparent consumer's attitude toward life. The best way for me to indicate this is to refer to a study made by a refugee scholar named Leo Lowenthal. He collected the popular biographies in magazines, such as *Colliers* and *The Saturday Evening Post,* for 1900 and for 1945 or 1946. Among the biographies of 1900 he found more of men of affairs and fewer of entertainers than in the later period. The entertainers treated at the turn of the century were more serious. The article writers of the time addressed their audiences by suggesting that if *you* can't do it, your son can. The emphasis was on success and achievement. The content revealed *how* a person became a success; it emphasized personal initiative and other personal traits that led to success. In the case of entertainers, there was more written about their technique and less about the way they consumed goods or used their leisure time. In 1945 and 1946, the popular biographies were different. Their emphasis was on swimming pools, on leisure life, on goods consumed. There were more entertainers and they were less serious in character; there were fewer men of affairs, fewer men of business, and even they were treated more as consumers of goods than as men who had accomplished and achieved. And it was usually ex-

63

plained that they had become a success by luck, by getting a good break.

Now this emphasis, so clearly marked in Lowenthal's studies, begins in the 1920's. In the 1920's there was a considerable investment in what we will call services, in culture and in entertainment. And if we look at these sociologically and economically, we can link them together. It was a time when new organizations—new publishing houses and new cultural enterprises—were established and capitalized, sometimes with millions and hundreds of millions of dollars. The motion pictures were expanded, and, in addition, the talking picture came into being. Radio became a major communications industry within a period of less than ten years. The Book-of-the-Month Club was founded, the Theater Guild was founded, a new kind of magazine—*Life*—was established.

Now, the writing of the 1920's is somewhat different from the writing of earlier periods of American life, and one of the defining differences is that the characters are presented more often in reference to consumption, in reference to leisure; they are more often seen at home, attempting to enjoy life. In this sense, there is even a marked difference between the earlier novels of Theodore Dreiser and his [1925] book, *An American Tragedy.* Dreiser, by the way, might be described as the American novelist who more than any other was influenced by the ideas of social Darwinism, which was a major tendency in American thought in the 1890's and early 1900's. But with the publication of *An American Tragedy* you can see a difference. The spectacle of grandeur and misery, the sense of survival of the fittest, the contrast of the strong and rich with the poor and weak, the dramatization of success and failure in Dreiser's early books—these are not to be found in *An American Tragedy.* In his earlier books, characters who were material successes in the world—Sister Carrie Meeber; Eugene Witla, the chief protaganist of Dreiser's [1915] novel, *The "Genius"*; and Frank Cowperwood, the hero of his trilogy, *The Titan, The Financier* and *The Stoic,* the first two books of which were published prior to 1920, the last posthumously—achieved their success as a consequence of some capacity, some trait, that the character himself or herself possessed. In the case of Witla, it was artistic talent; in the case of Cowperwood, financial wizardry; in the case of Carrie Meeber, a warmth and sympathy of nature that helps her to become an actress, which is the basis for her success. But Clyde Griffith, the chief protaganist of *An American Tragedy,* is not only a failure; he cannot apply his best talents. His boyhood is socially abnormal; and his first contact with the outer world is in a hotel, where he is a busboy. Dreiser stresses this; as a matter of fact, you might say that, particularly for an earlier generation of Americans, there was a kind of hotel culture. The hotel was a kind of fraternity and country club of the self-made, uneducated man, of salesmen and others. There they learned their manners and got an idea of how the other half lived. Clyde Griffith, seeing the way people who to him are rich and successful live in the hotel where he works, seeing the way they waste money, gains a distorted sense of values. But again, it is a distorted sense of values in relationship to *spending* money, not to *making* it, to consumption and leisure, not to achievement. In the end, the emphasis is on success by connection. The rich in *An American Tragedy* are treated entirely in terms of leisure and consumption. I'm emphasizing this because we can see the degree to which today this kind of attitude permeates our education and our national life.

That is one of the aspects of the 1920's. And if you consider a number of the writers of that period—F. Scott Fitzgerald, Ernest Hemingway, Ring Lardner—you will find that it is an important one. If you ask yourself the question, "What types of occupations, what types of work are described in the short stories of Ring Lardner?" for example, you will find that every character who works works at a job that caters to the amusement of others: he is a golf caddy, a songwriter, a ballplayer. Consider the world of Ernest Hemingway—and I'm making a descriptive statement: It is a tourists' world, a world of Americans in Europe on a vacation; or it is the world of newspapermen, like that of the "I" of *The Sun Also Rises*. I think you will find the same emphasis in the movies and in the commercial or popular stories. All this represents the beginning of a change in the conception of the American way of life.

That is one of the important features of the 1920's. It has nothing to do with the present way of interpretating writers in terms of myths and symbols that are archetypes, that have some universal significance.

A second important feature of the 1920's that is neglected today is the depth and the significance of postwar disillusionment. In 1916 Woodrow Wilson was elected, largely on the slogan "He Kept Us out of War." In 1917 the United States entered the first World War. The liberals of the time believed, with Wilson, that this was a war to make the world safe for democracy. They believed that the war would be *their* war—that, as a consequence of it, a more liberal and more democratic world could be created. After the Versailles Treaty of Peace, disillusionment set in, and original studies of the origins of the First World War began to be made in the United States. One of these, a book that influenced the new generation of the time, was *The Economic Consequences of the Peace,* which was an attack on the Versailles Treaty. And the generation of writers that had gone to war and the newer generation that had not were both strongly infected with a kind of bitterness and sense of disillusionment expressed in this and other books about the war. One of the first novels of John Dos Passos was *Three Soldiers,* a novel of war disillusionment in which the soldiers are ground down by an army machine. Ernest Hemingway was largely interpreted as a novelist of postwar disillusionment; when Gertrude Stein said to him, "You are a lost generation," a phrase he quoted in the front of his first novel, *The Sun Also Rises,* she was referring to the fact of a generation that had suffered such spiritual wounds from war that it became directionless. And it is interesting, what with current interpretations of Hemingway, to note that "I" of *The Sun Also Rises* is impotent because of ruins of war; that kind of symbolism is too obvious and too definitely intended to please the critics who come later to invent meanings and significance in the writers of the 20's.

But writers like Hemingway and Dos Passos were not the dominating writers of the 20's. The influential voices were those of the older generation, of Dreiser, George Jean Nathan, Sinclair Lewis, Sherwood Anderson and, to some degree, Carl Sandburg, Edgar Lee Masters and James Branch Cabell. These were writers who had begun to publish their first books in the 1910's, or between 1910 and 1920, and they were directly or indirectly influenced by the 1890's in England—by the *fin de siecle,* or the Yellow Decade, as it is called—that is, by the time of the period of the break-up of the Victorian world.

In the 1920's, some of the *fin de siecle* English writers—Wilde and Shaw, George Moore and William Butler Yeats—became more popular in America. And the city became the landscape of their ideas and dreams—a significant center of culture, of art, of esthetic experience. From the 1890's on in the United States, we had the triumph of the town over the country and of the city over the small town. This is reflected in the first novel of Theodore Dreiser, *Sister Carrie,* the opening pages of which tell us of a country girl from a small town in Indiana going to the big city to find a better type of life, more life, and to make her fortune in a bigger world.

The city was a bigger world. In the early novels of Dreiser, every town to which a character goes, and in particular Chicago, represents a sense of hope, of buildings going up, of new neighborhoods. And of course Dreiser himself felt very strongly the spirit of growth in Chicago when he first went there. He said that Chicago was singing and that he was singing with it.

Now, then, by the 1920's the city had triumphed over the town and there is an attack on the small town. There had been earlier novels that reflected a kind of disillusionment with the small town—*The Damnation of Theron Ware,* for example. But in the 1920's there was a strong revulsion expressed, in criticism and in imaginative writing, of the small town—and thus, by the way, of the origins of the writers themselves. Floyd Dell wrote a minor novel, *Moon Calf,* a novel of the small-town boy going to the big city. Sinclair Lewis's first success, *Main Street,* was to a considerable extent an attack on the small town; the main character, Carol Kennicott, cannot have a more cultured life or more personally meaningful life in a small town of Minnesota that is located, perhaps, near Minneapolis. And in *Babbitt,* Zenith, the "zip city," is actually Minneapolis, but is presented as though it were a smaller town.

At the same time, you find in this attack on the small town that the revulsion against it is felt largely in terms of the way people enjoy life—of what they feel about the goods of life and, once again, of the values of their leisure and consumption time. In respect to this it would be interesting to compare, say, a salesman in Sinclair Lewis with the salesman, Charles Drouet, who is Carrie's first lover and one of the leading characters in *Sister Carrie.*

Now, along with the small town, there was, in the 1920's, an attack on puritanism, which Dreiser and H.L. Menken helped to lead. The kind of puritanism they attacked was mainly a colonial, Victorian puritanism with an emphasis on sin; it took the form of a verbal revulsion against sin and led to efforts to legislate other people's morals and other people's conduct. Puritanism was, of course, a much bigger and more complicated phenomenon than that, and the effect of puritanism in England, particularly of the nonconformist sects, was different: English Puritanism created a moral attitude toward work, for instance, and stimulated scientists like Faraday. There was a certain constructive, moral feature to English Puritanism that was different from the small-town, rather parochial puritanism that Mencken and Lewis and Dreiser attacked.

In the 1920's, one of the significant facts of life was the city. The city had become so important that rural life was laughed at, and the farm problem and other rural problems were considered almost inconsequential. Although there's no necessary correlation between the facts, it is interesting to note that the one group in America who did not participate in the prosperity of the country in the 1920's was the farmers. The emphasis was on the city; even though Mencken's main object of attack was Prohibition, for example, Mencken himself recognized that in this attack he was also attacking the moral attitude of small towns and rural areas and their attempt to legislate morality.

Another aspect of life in the 1920's was the feeling of desire, and even of zest, for personal freedom. Insofar as there was revolt of any kind in the twenties, it was revolt in the name of self-expression. One of the things that made Sherwood Anderson so important was that self-expression, self-realization, was so involved in his writing. His third book, *Winesburg, Ohio,* published in 1919, was the most influential of his books. It is a series of related short stories set in a small Ohio town in the 1890's—probably Camden, Ohio, near Cincinnati, where Anderson was born. Now, the humor of America had been a humor directed against every kind of oddity, every peculiarity, every sort of person who did not fit into the middle-class, Protestant, Nordic, Anglo-Saxon norm. Accent, brogue, the color of your skin, the shape of your nose, the peculiarity of writing poetry or reading books— these were the objects of humor. The people who were queer were the people who didn't fit the norm. Now, Sherwood Anderson subtitled his book "A Book of Grotesqueries" and every one of the characters of *Winesburg, Ohio,* is singular or queer in some sense. The pattern of most of the stories is one in which there is a sudden awakening of creative feeling in a character; but because that creative feeling has hitherto been damned up, the awakening takes some aberrant, or neurotic, or violent, or aggressive form of expression. The notion of creativity, and of the capacity for creativity in everyone, is central in Sherwood Anderson, and that aspect of his work was seen and appreciated in the 1920's.

I've spoken about the small town and the country. Anderson wrote about the small town and the country in a different way from Dreiser and Lewis; he wrote without sarcasm, without irony, without making a direct attack. He wrote about them with a kind of remembered humanity that took into account the frustration of people living in small towns. Anderson had grown up in the 1890's, a period of great hope in American capitalism. It was a period of solidification of big and sometimes huge monopolies. It was a period in which factories spread to the small towns and crafts began to disappear. The feeling of craftsmanship was strong in Anderson; he had abiding memories of craftsmen, and of the changes that had been wrought in American life and had brought their destruction.

Now, Anderson read very few books, and I don't believe that he ever read the work of Thorstein Veblen. Veblen was one of the most profound and important of American social thinkers. I'm inclined to think that, in many ways, he was an advance on Karl Marx as a contributor to social science. Veblen's book, *The Instinct of Workmanship,* was different from the "instinct psychology" of the time. It was influenced by men like John Dewey and, I believe, William James. Veblen saw the "instinct of workmanship" as, really, the need to create. With that, he saw how the organization of the life of man by time in the development of the factory system distorted and thwarted human nature. Sherwood Anderson's stories are a kind of illustration of Veblen's analysis of the effects of industrial civilization on the nature of man and the instinct of workmanship as Veblen described them.

Similarly, Anderson never read the American philosophers Dewey and George Herbert Mead. I am thinking particularly of Mead here, of the idea of social identity he expressed. Mead was influenced by the American sociologist Charles Cooley, who used the phrase "the looking glass self" to describe the way in which, in looking at others in a society, we see ourselves. Mead developed this idea of "the looking glass self" into a conception of the way the self, or the personality, is created in society; and so Mead's social psychology can be seen to apply to the problem of what we will call "identity." Now, as I suggested, Anderson was seeking his own identity in a world that had changed from the world of his boyhood, and in some sense his search can be seen also as an illustration of Mead's ideas. In any case, Anderson is significant for the reason that, with the changes that had been wrought in America—with the triumph of the town over the country and of the big town over the small town—the problem of identity was a significant one at the time when he was writing.

There was another side of the 1920's. In those days there was a separation between literary men and political and philosophical thinkers. As a matter of fact, many of the writers, and particularly of the new generation of Hemingway and Glenway Wescott and F. Scott Fitzgerald and others, did not read much of the political writing of the day. Still, the other side of the 1920's is important, and it is well described in *The Crisis of the Old Order,* the first volume of Arthur M. Schlesinger, Jr.'s biography of Franklin Delano Roosevelt. In it Arthur Schlesinger shows the preparation for the New Deal that took place in the 1920's—the thinking about social problems, about problems of taxation, problems of bigness in industry, problems of social justice and social control. In all the major universities there were professors and students who became the shock troops, as it were, of the New Deal. In most contemporary pictures of the 1920's, this side of the time is not recognized, partly because it is so little reflected in the novels of the day, but there was intense social and political thought. Columbia University Professor Raymond Moley more or less suggests that the New Deal was pieced together as an election strategy, but this is not true; Roosevelt gathered around him the men who had done new and original social thinking in the previous decade, and this was how the New Deal was prepared.

To some degree, literary men like H.L. Mencken, who could not stand Roosevelt after 1934, also helped to create the generation of New Dealers. Mencken's attack on bigness, his attack on businessmen and on political figures like Coolidge and Harding, helped to prepare New Deal journalists and others. So, although Mencken was one of the most bitter critics of the New Deal, he himself contributed to it.

I've taken up and attempted to present to you various aspects of the 1920's. I do not think that you can choose as your subject the life of a country and its generations throughout ten years of change and then lock it up with one or two stereotyped descriptions. There were many features of the 1920's. And the past is not fixed. The past is always changing. We can now see more of the meaning of the 1920's than we could twenty years ago, and one of the meanings we can see is this: I mentioned the beginning of a "consumption" attitude. I mentioned Sherwood Anderson, the small town, the changes in America in the 1890's. But the decisive change in the small town came with the railroads. When the economic life of the small town was no longer based on carts and horses but was based on the railroad, the possibility or material basis of trade brands and of national markets was created. One factor in the change of life in the small town was the introduction of the trade brand. After the 1920's America had reached the phase—which was interrupted by the Depression—wherein it was sufficiently rich so that the goods of life could be spread widely. The goods of life were spread widely in the 1920's—and after the Second World War prosperity was spread much further. And then there were new media of communication, which have by now made possible "a war of the trade brands," in which the consumer emphasis can be seen most strongly.

The fact that we have television and have it operated as it is has given those who do the advertising a growing control over American culture. Now, there is a difference between the treatment of leisure and consumption in stories and the manipulation of culture in order to practice what is called "hidden persuasion" and sell goods. In the 1920's there was a protest against bigness; I mean that hundreds of leading writers and millions of others protested against it. The bigness that was attacked then has survived; it has survived in the consumption industries, and it has survived to the degree that other tendencies seem, at the moment at least, to be defeated.

I began by stating the problem of America continually growing up and coming of age. It's meaningless to say this of any one period. But if my comments and analysis are correct, we see in the 1920's the process of a changing consciousness in America, a changing consciousness in relation to changing social and economic and political conditions. There is never a change in one field only. In the 1920's there was originality and creativity of both social and political thought, and there was originality and creativity in the writing of the time. And I would emphasize this: The twenties are significant, not only because there is criticism in this creativity, but because in it we can date the beginning of a new kind of emphasis and attitude in America. After 1918, leisure was a mass problem and not a class problem. I mentioned Thorstein Veblen, whose first book, *The Theory of the Leisure Class,* published in 1899, was an attack on the rich; it presented the rich as a kind of aristocracy—as a class of people who had developed a culture, developed habits, of conspicuous consumption—a phrase still used quite frequently today—because they wanted to show that they had nothing they had to do.

Well, by the 1920's many people had more leisure, had much time in which they had nothing they had to do. Today this is more pronounced yet; and the conspicuous consumption of the turn of the century became conforming consumption from the twenties to the fifties.

Now, in ways like these we can see the beginning of changes in American conditions and in American consciousness of them. Where they are going to end we do not know. But if we look back we can say that the 1920's were one of the germinating periods of

71

change, of all-sided change in American life. If the time is studied in this way, and if we recognize that there are many tendencies and influences at play, we will perhaps gain more insight than if we hunt for stereotypes, as some of the literary and other critics are doing at the present time.

Ed Lanson on Nietzsche

"I'll prove eternal recurrence to you now," Ed went on.

"That's a big order, Ed," John Delafield said.

"I don't claim any originality in proving it. What I say is Nietzsche, not me. I'm only a humble seeker, and I found this object of my search in his vineyard, if I may indulge in a figure of speech. He knew about the law of the conservation of energy. . . . According to the law of the conservation of energy, no energy is lost." He turned to Ellen. "That means that when we die, the energy that constitutes us is not lost. It changes. In the case of beautiful girls like you and Catherine Anne, that energy probably becomes flowers, flowers that the lovers of a future May will pick."

Watching Ellen, Ed did not see Catherine Anne wince and try to hide her feelings with a pathetic smile. John Delafield looked at him impatiently.

"But persons like myself, their energy will probably turn into onions."

"But what does that prove?" John Delafield asked.

"I don't believe that. I am a Catholic," Catherine Anne said.

Ellen Rogers

"What is important is that . . . we defend sincerity and honesty in writing, and defend the sovereignty of the artist and the writer over their materials . . ."

New Writing and Young Writers

Speech delivered at the University of Minnesota, Minneapolis,
February 8, 1954

The other night we talked about Ernest Hemingway, and there was some question of interpretation of Hemingway's work. There was a question about whether or not he tried to use a language of the "fifth dimension," and we didn't know exactly what the fifth dimension meant; we couldn't discuss it. There was a question of whether or not Hemingway, along with William Faulkner, represented a new trend in American literature, a trend which utilized myths and allegories. I was thinking then, and I've been thinking since, that there was a time, when Ernest Hemingway was a young writer, when he was described as representative of a new generation. This generation was considered to be "the lost generation." The phrase came from Gertrude Stein, who made a remark, apparently to Hemingway and others: "You are a lost generation." Hemingway quoted that remark, if I remember correctly, at the front of *The Sun Also Rises*.

Thinking of this, I think of a more general question about interpretation. In the 1920's Ernest Hemingway was considered to be a representative of youth and despair, of youth giving voice to a postwar reaction of disillusionment. The other night I qualified that characterization by pointing out that theirs was disillusionment in reflection, after the first postwar years, at the best time in the 1920's, at a period when it seemed as though there was going to be a restabilization of the world.

In the 1930's, however, Hemingway came to be seen, even by some of his admirers, such as Malcolm Cowley, as a writer who was decadent. The word "decadent" wasn't used by Cowley, but Cowley discovered that Hemingway lacked a positive feeling. Another writer said the same thing more strongly when he said that Hemingway lacked social consciousness in facing the proletariat. In the thirties, because of a Marxist trend in criticism, a trend that was expressed noisily although usually with a great deal of vulgarity and insensibility to literature, Ernest Hemingway seemed to be on the way down. He has now been rediscovered by a new generation of young critics. According to them he is creating a new dimension in language, and he is

74

creating myths and symbols and allegories. I mention this as a kind of warning—as a warning that we shouldn't become overly excited about a particular critical tendency of the moment, and that we should have a certain caution about accepting such a tendency as a definitive one. The history of literary criticism is full of overstatements and of varying interpretations; if you attempt to evaluate a writer by means of the critical writings about him you are going to become very confused.

Before Ernest Hemingway began to write there was another generation, and the young writers within it gave voice to hope and aspiration. One of them was Randolph Bourne. Randolph Bourne was one of the finest liberal spirits in this country in the early years of the twentieth century. He was a humpback, a man very disfigured; but he had an almost shining purity of spirit. Before the First World War, when he was in his twenties, he felt that he was the spokesman for his generation. He was influenced by the ideas and philosophy of John Dewey, and he saw his generation as one moving toward freedom, the future as moving toward a conquest by youth, toward a time in which this country would be freer. He was disillusioned by the support that a great section of the liberal intelligentsia gave to the First World War, and he wrote two very disillusioned but quite brilliant essays about it.

Then I think of the younger generation of the thirties. In 1930, *The Saturday Review* held an essay contest for writers thirty years old and under. Their essays were supposed to point the direction for the next generation. The contest was won by a younger writer named William Harlan Hale, and in his prize-winning essay William Harlan Hale declared he was of the opinion that all of the hard battles and necessary conquests in American literature had been fought and won; that American literature was safe from philistinism and from censorship; and that American letters would go on to a new period of affirmation.

Now, younger spokesmen, younger writers of a new generation, and critics are always looking at new work, the work of youth, in order to find some new trend. Critics tend to look at decades in the same way. At the beginning and end of each decade, literary magazines and supplements attempt to get essays and articles that describe the spirit of the decade, and fixed clichés about decades are implanted on many minds. With each new generation, there is a cry to find a representitive someone to express either hope or despair; either affirmation or negation. In this discussion of younger writers today, I am not going to find either hope or despair, affirmation or negation in my references to what I have read of them. And I am going to repeat my warning that it is very easy to overestimate and overvalue a new school of writing, and to be deceived by interpretive tendencies of the present moment—to take the so-called "new critics," for example, with too much seriousness.

Leaving pulse-feeling aside, then, I'll begin by making reference to an essay that appeared in *New World Writing* No. 5. Most of you probably know what *New World Writing* is. For those who don't, it is a paperbacked anthology, issued four times a year, I believe, by the New American Library, which is very hospitable to new writing and younger writers and has printed extracts of novels and stories of a great many well-known younger writers in America. There is an article in *New World Writing* No. 5 signed "Libra." It was written by one of the younger writers, and in it he attacks all past writing—he attacks most of the critics, F. Scott Fitzgerald, etc. He points out that the new writers—and he mentions only three of them: Tennessee Williams, Paul Bowles and Carson McCullers—have been able to face life's darkness and despair in a way no writers of the past have been able to do. He claims that these writers are more courageous than writers of the past and that they are misunderstood by critics. The article was called "Ladders to Heaven." Through their courageous facing of blackest and darkest despair, they find their particular "Ladders to Heaven." A curious and very interesting thing about this essay is this: Whenever, or almost whenever, a critic or a writer attempts to praise a book he likes, and particularly when he attempts to praise a friend, and does so by denigrating other writers, and particularly by denigrating whole groups and generations and knocking reputations over with one fell swoop, he usually creates antagonism. This young writer, in his article "Ladders to Heaven," does a disservice to the three writers whom he praises—Paul Bowles, Carson McCullers and Tennessee Williams—because, when a reader is told that no writer of the past has been as good or as brave as they are, the reader will naturally feel angry and defensive.

If we go back to our old terms of affirmation and negation, "Libra" emphasizes negation. I said that I was not going to feel pulses or to interpret writers by whether they are affirmative or negative. But there is among a number of newer writers an inclination to present the neurotic victim, or negative character, as the hero or the chief protaganist of the work. I do not know whether this suggests a major trend, and I don't know precisely how to interpret it; I don't know to what degree it grows out of the contemporary interest in psychoanalysis and Freud. Still, I am going to make a few general remarks that I hope may have some bearing on the subject.

You may recall that in my first lecture to you I mentioned that there had been a somewhat pronounced change in America after the First World War. I pointed out that there had come to be a greater emphasis on leisure in our literature and in American culture as a whole, and I illustrated my remarks with references to the different heroes in Theodore Dreiser. Now, in our own last ten years there have been tremendous changes in the world. We have had the bloodiest world war in history. We've had the discovery of the atomic bomb, and then of the hydrogen bomb. We've had the recrudescence of authoritarianism, not only in the last ten years, but for the last twenty or thirty. We have lived through a period that was neither peace nor war—a cold war. We have had a constant series of alarms. And now we have a new generation of writers, one that has come out of a different world from the world that those of us who are older emerged from. In some ways it is a more frightening world, even though it is at least temporarily more secure from poverty and war. Young writers have not had anything like the economic struggles that an older generation of writers had; to my knowledge, at least, none of them has had to go to work as a common laborer, as Theodore Dreiser at one time did, nor has any met with the difficulties of the public attack on moral grounds that Dreiser met with. They do not have the same difficulty in getting publishers to print their work, so that, as far as gaining exposure, and in some instances, gaining recognition and making money is concerned, it has been easier for them. But in terms of the character of the age in which we live, the suppressed and half suppressed fight, the possibility for an increase in anxiety—in those terms their tasks are more difficult than the tasks of earlier writers, and they have to assimilate experience that all of us are assimilating slowly and that none of us understands too well. I think that psychologically it may be more difficult for them then it has been for us.

This may or may not be the reason why there is this tendency to present the neurotic victim as hero. There is a related question that I would pose but will not try to answer, and it is this: To what degree do younger writers represent the life of America, and to what degree do the feelings, and the hopes and aspirations, and the fears and despair of Americans flow through these writers and their work? I don't know, but I think it is a good question to keep in mind as we proceed.

I would like to make some reference to a few specific writers. The author of "Ladders to Heaven" mentioned Paul Bowles. One of Bowles's books, which is available in a reprint edition, is called, I believe, *The Sheltering Sky*. It's the story of three Americans in Africa—a husband, a wife and a friend. It's written in the first person, and the friend is telling the story. There is a feeling of a kind of dessication to it, a kind of purposelessness among the characters, that indicates despair far deeper than any despair you may see in or deduce from Ernest Hemingway's *The Sun Also Rises*. *The Sheltering Sky* has been described as representing the attitudes of the new "lost generation," a generation more lost than any previous one. I don't know if this is so. I can say this: Paul Bowles impresses me as a writer of extraordinary talents. At the same time, there is a lack of affirmation of the people in his book—of feeling for the girl who, separated from her husband by some accident, some misconnection, finally practically goes crazy. There is a lack of feeling for all the characters, at least in the sense that you will find it in the work of many earlier writers. It is a book of tremendous talent and of dessicated feelings.

Now, it's possible to draw some parallel between *The Sheltering Sky* and the work of two other, younger writers—Calder Willingham and Norman Mailer. I have read two of Calder Willingham's books; as a matter of fact I happen to be largely responsible for his success, since a review of mine was what started him off. His first book was *End As a Man,* and it tells the story of a group of boys living in a military academy in the South, in Virginia. There is a great deal of cruelty in the work; the attitude of the authorities of the school toward the young cadets is strictly disciplinary, one in which there is no concern for their humanity; they are being educated to be cogs in a machine, and being educated also in a kind of sadism. There is sadism among the students themselves—violation of the southern code of gentlemanliness, and so on. A number of people have criticized me for liking the book, but I reread it after I was criticized and found, on the second reading, that it has an extraordinary power—it is a negative picture of aspects and values of the South.

After that book, Willingham wrote a second novel, called *Geraldine Bradshaw,* which is the story of two young men and their efforts to seduce a girl in Chicago. The opening three or four or five chapters show a rare talent. One of the two young men is a bellboy, and in those first chapters the reader gets a very good sense of a big hotel—a hotel like the Palmer House. In passing, it is interesting to note that this young bellboy is strikingly different from Dreiser's bellboy, Clyde Griffith, in *An American Tragedy*; in Willingham's bellboy, there is no sense of wonder or bewilderment, no lack of at least superficial sophistication, as there was in Griffith. In any case, after the first few chapters, the book fades away in talk. The attitude toward sex and toward women is very unpleasant; there is a lot of talk that would seem to be profound, but it is merely youthful boastfulness, and it gets nowhere. You can't see it as a book that emphasizes potential values in humanity. It is a book that is negativistic in spirit.

In the same way, Norman Mailer's novel, *The Naked and the Dead*. There is a pattern in that book that runs more or less like this: Those who are educated and those who have some kind of political awareness are more sensitive than those who do not. The soldiers in the novel all are treated negatively. All that is seen of them are their brutalities and their alleged inclination to talk about women in obscenities. Strikingly, in this book and in a number of these books, there is a certain distrust of women—a difference from older writers in the treatment of women and girls. It would be interesting to contrast the treatment of women by Dreiser, Sinclair Lewis and Sherwood Anderson with that by some of these young writers.

A writer who is strikingly different from these three is Leonard Bishop. He has begun to have censorship troubles. He has written two novels. One is called *Down All Your Streets* and the other is called *Made For Love. Down All Your Streets* was published about two years ago. It is the story of a family on the East Side of New York, and is about eight hundred pages long. It is about two hundred pages too long. In a certain sense it is ultra-realism. If a character is going to make a telephone call, for instance, he would take the money out of his pocket and you would be told that he had a quarter, a nickel and a dime, then the number of steps he took to the telephone booth in a restaurant would be described, the tables therein and what was on the tables; you would learn that he was opening the door of the booth, that he was closing the door, that he was dialing and what number; a buzzing would be described, and then the character would start to talk. This is a parody, but not much of one; every scene is described with as much detail, and much of it unnecessary. It slows down the book.

But the striking thing about *Down All Your Streets* is this: Unlike some of the other writers I've mentioned, Bishop is able to identify with the whole range of his varied characters. He identifies with a Jewish business man, with his wife, with two young sons of a man who is a derelict and a dope fiend, with the dope fiend, with the wife of the dope fiend. There is a great deal of power in this. There is a capacity to get inside people and so to identify them, so to describe them, that, in the passages describing the need of the derelictal man for dope, for instance, I felt, and I think it possible others may have felt, that the man ought to get it. One hopes he gets his dope. That kind of power to create character—that's one of the things that make a writer, and that make a writer great.

Bishop's second novel, *Made For Love,* is more sensational. It is the story of two men who are Jewish. One of them was born in the old country, and his wife calls him a foreigner because she has been born here. For years he has worked as a clerk in a store. Then a friend of his, a promoter who had been a soldier with him in the First World War, gets him to go into a charity racket in which they raise money for churches, for organizations doing good, and take most of the profit. There is a wonderfully vivid description of the process by which they con people; in places called "boiler rooms" they get telephone men to make telephone calls, saying that they're priests of parishes or commanders of American Legion posts, and they talk people into making contributions and take the greater percentage of profit for themselves. Still, the book is highly sensational—there is a very sensational homosexual scene in it—and it doesn't have the solid power of Bishop's first book.

I do not think that Bishop displays as much skill as a man like Paul Bowles, and I don't think that *any* young American writer has more talent than Calder Willingham. But there is a difference in Bishop; he is able to identify with more of life than they are. I don't say that this is good or bad in itself, particularly because I'm speaking of writers who have written one, two or three books in their late twenties and early thirties. I don't believe we should make final and definitive judgments about them.

If, for instance, you contrast Flaubert and Tolstoy in the same way, you would find that Tolstoy was able to write about more kinds of people than Flaubert was. If you take a certain type of character in Tolstoy, say, an Army officer, you will find many varieties of the type. There is more than one kind of general, more than one kind of bureaucrat, more than one kind of housewife. There is a greater variation within classes and groups than in Flaubert. In Flaubert there are relatively few characters, treated with great intensity.

Of course, this doesn't mean that Flaubert was not a great writer. There is no point in claiming that Flaubert was greater than Tolstoy or vice versa. Similarly, when I present this contrast between Leonard Bishop and Bowles and Willingham, I am not making a judgment.

I'd like to make a brief reference to another contemporary writer, a writer whom the man signing himself "Libra" also praised—Carson McCullers. I've read two of her books—*A Member of the Wedding* and *The Heart is a Lonely Hunter. The Heart is a Lonely Hunter* is, to my mind, an extremely warm and human book. There is something very interesting to me in it. It is this: It is one of the best pictures of a girl growing up that I've read in Amercan writing. You know, for every story of a girl growing up, for every story of a girl going into adolescence and her teens, there are perhaps fifty or one hundred stories of the development of boys into men. You get a sense of the early development of a girl in *The Heart is a Lonely Hunter.* It's also true that there is a feeling of sympathy in the author's treatment of exceptional and odd types—of people who are singular, who don't fit easily into patterns. It's a mark of the humanity of that book that you find this in it.

Many years ago the German Marxist Rosa Luxembourg wrote an article about the Russian writer Kovalenko, and in it she said that in Russian writing you find again and again that there is sympathy for the person who is a victim, and most sympathy for the person who is most victimized. That is an interesting comment and an illuminating insight into Russian literature; but in passing let me say that Miss Luxembourg's Marxist bias then came into play and she made some gratuitous remarks, denigrating Baudelaire as a decadent. The humanity I find in Carson McCuller's work is the same kind of humanity that I find in Sherwood Anderson's. In Anderson's writing, it is the people who are odd whom he treats with most sympathy.

Now in the case of Paul Bowles and Calder Willingham and Norman Mailer, there is a different attitude at work; I mean there is an attitude, one that I see, anyway, of hatred—of violent, rebellious dissent in Mailer and to some degree in Willingham. In Bowles there is more the appearance of interest. Now, is this writing good or is it bad? Possibly it is something that is evolving. The time has brought forth some writers of unmistakeable talent. I don't think that anyone who is sensitive to literature would deny that a writer like Bowles has talent, that he is an artist. And so I'm going to leave things as they are here and leave you to judge, as you will or if you wish, if and when you read these books.

Now, with these things in mind, I'm going to make a few remarks. In the past there was Greenwich Village. In the later 1910's and early 1920's, Greenwich Village had a positive as well as a negative significance. It was a real place for writers to go and to congregate. The Bohemian sections of Chicago, and then of New York, were the places where Anderson, Dreiser, Masters, Edna St. Vincent Millay and a number of other writers of worth and distinction met. They were a means of escape, places where an artistic milieu had been created. Greenwich Village was not merely a place for posers; there was place in it for many serious persons who wanted to write and who did write, who had gone out and found a world in which they belonged.

It died; Bohemia died its natural death and can't be restored. We are living in different times and in different circumstances. Today the academy, the university, has become the center to which writers are attracted. I spoke of how a large number of earlier American writers were self-educated and had little relationship to the university. I also pointed out that a large number of professsors in those days—most of the English department people—set themselves against this writing, and in some cases—I mentioned one, Professor Doty of Texas—considered it to be downright unpatriotic. During the First World War, realism, as a matter of fact, was considered by some of these people to be pro-German.

The universities have changed; and newer writers are looking to them for support, are working in them. Universities are among the major publishers. Now, this is a change in the social conditions of writing and has become part of the milieu of the writer of today. Along with it, there has been a revolution in publishing. Today publishing is big business. The reprint books—and there are something like 250 million paperback reprint books sold a year—have, in effect, marked a new era in the publishing industry. We now have a mass market in books. To date, younger writers have been received with hospitality, and their works have been published; there are at least three paperback anthologies that are receptive to young writers, to the writers I've named and others, and in some instances they've had considerable sales. And so, as this revolution has taken place, I would not say that the hospitality of the industry to writing has necessarily become less than it ever was. As a matter of fact, I think that, editorially, there is more hospitality to serious and honest work—particularly if it is work that violates conventional, puritanical standards—than there was in the early 1900's. There are problems, however, that are going to be created by the presence of big business in literature; because, whereas certain large reprint publishers, and particularly the New American Library, have shown great taste and openness, it doesn't matter to many of the big reprint publishers whether they have one writer or another—they'll bid for him, but they'll make their profits regardless of him or of any particular writer. In this sense, there is a likelihood that the writer will become less important.

There is a need for a certain kind of militancy today; for determination to hold out against a subtle corruption of values that can accompany the growing bigness of the literary book industry. But even as I say this, I would add that, although there have been many recent efforts to censor books and particularly to censor reprint books, until now the reprint publishers have shown real spirit and have fought the censors.

I have touched on some of the conditions under which writing is being done today. I don't know how writing will develop or what direction it is going to take; quite frequently the prophets who say they know are proved wrong. In any case, I think it's not so important whether writing will take one or another direction; I think what is important is that after the writing has been done, the writing be kept free; that we defend sincerity and honesty in writing and defend the sovereignty of the artist and the writer over their own materials. I think it is important that efforts be made to establish as much clarity as possible in the literary world, and in criticism, and in the reception of books. I think that is more important. And I would emphasize again that, particularly with younger writers in a period like ours, when we are all attempting to absorb things that we don't understand, it is best that we be a little bit less than harsh in making our judgments, even of negativity in writing. We should see perhaps that some members of the younger generation are attempting to work out how they and people like them feel about a world that is changing, and that is more dangerous than the current prosperity of America would cause us to believe.

I'll stop now with the hope that in the discussion and questions we will bring out some further points, and that when you question me, you question me on points about which you don't think I've been clear or you think I'm wrong.

Thank you, Mr. Farrell. Our discussion tonight will be led by Dr. Ralph Ross, Professor of Humanities at the University of Minnesota. Dr. Ross.

You probably all know the story of the man who goes to the psychiatrist and when asked what his trouble is says simply that he is very fond of potato pancakes. The psychiatrist responds that this isn't exactly an illness. The patient says, "Yes, but I just love potato pancakes." And the psychiatrist says, "Well, I love potato pancakes, too." "Why," the patient asked eagerly—"do you too keep them in a trunk?"

Now, for some strange reason, we learn constantly of all the plays and novels people have that are kept in trunks. And perhaps the love for the American novel is best exhibited by the number of novels that are kept in trunks, in attics, in basements and so on—all the published and unpublished books, plenty of which, by the way, are sent to publishers ultimately, if not by the writers' own hands. Shortly after the end of the last war, the writing courses and work-

shops, so-called, in the large universities, were flooded, especially with young men on the G.I. Bill who wanted to learn to write. They got out of the Army deciding that this above all was what they wanted to do. Whether or not they wanted to write or, just having been in the Army and having been as regimented as they were for so long, wanted to lead as independent a life as they could conceive— and that of the creative artist is probably such a life—I don't know. But the demand for these courses still continues. I just got a bulletin from a school in the city of New York, the New School for Social Research, announcing fourteen new writing workshops, taught, I'm sorry to say, by critics.

If Mr. Farrell will forgive me, I'm going to continue in a vein very different from his. The path of a writer, after all, is to keep his eye on the object, and the path of the professor, I suppose, is to keep his head in the clouds. In any event, it is a kind of occupational disease; we critics can't help generalizing or asking why, can't help expecting an answer to the generalization—despite the fact that, in terms of an acute eye on the object, there may be no such answer reasonably forthcoming.

In our day, you know, there has been a tremendous clamor on the part of some critics who claim that we are going to witness the death struggle of the novel. The age of the novel, they tell us, is almost over. One very distinguished critic, Lionel Trilling, has been on both sides of this question at various times in his career. He never puts it very strongly, but he thinks the thing's about to die or it will survive; his last opinion, as I recall it, was that the modern works of art will hold everything, he thinks; this leads him to realize that it ought to die. The reason for this argument has been, presumably, that the novel is middle-class art, that it arose with the growth of the bourgeois; that the theater died with the coming of the bourgeois, and that the theater was essentially aristocratic art; proletarian art, in a totally new form—as the novel was a totally new form—has not yet been created. All that has happened is that, as the middle class has invaded the theater and so writes Broadway plays, the proletariat has invaded the novel and so often writes bad novels. But this middle-class art is about to die because the middle class is in its death agony.

*There's a young critic from Vermont, by the name of Aldridge, whom you may know of. He had a great period of success; his first book—and he was then a boy in his mid-twenties—was reviewed on the first page of the **New York Times Sunday Book Review**, and that warrants a great paraphrase. If you haven't seen the book, I'm sure you'll enjoy this paraphrase very much. He said, "The subject of* *the novel is manners. Americans can no longer write novels because there aren't any manners except in those tiny civilized communities with tradition. I refer," he said, "of course, to the deep South and to Boston, Massachusetts. All the rest of the United States," and I think I am going to quote this exactly, "is an arid, cultural Midwest, in which people can scarcely be said to live." Well, eh, some of our barely living Midwesterners have, in their own time, produced some things that look a little like novels. one wonders where Fitzgerald, for example, got his background, living neither in Boston nor the deep South. But if these things are true at all, or even if they're not true, there is some vague correctness in assuming that the novel somehow did arise with the middle class and was, for some time at least, concerned with the manners, habits and destiny of the middle class. What can we say about the writer's imaginative response as a kind of growth? To what extent can we classify any of these people? This again is the occupational disease from which we suffer. It seems to me that people like Paul Bowles, Carson McCullers, and Tennessee Williams—the three writers whom Mr. Farrell mentions first—do have, as he pointed out, one thing in common, a concern with the neurotic victim as hero. Now I wonder if it isn't the case—and even as I go along with the generalization that has been made, I'm going to falter and put it somewhat in the form of a question—if it isn't the case that Bowles, especially, as the extraordinarily talented man he is, has found a replacement for the old novel of Gothic horror, with a new novel of neurotic horror? And although the others aren't really too horrible—McCullers the least of the three, although her characters always have some kind of deformation, in some way—I wonder whether the mood in the soul of the character replaces the horrors that used to come from outside, and whether what we have now is not so much anything new as a twist, a new way of doing something that is very old. And that is quite the fact: did Bowles produce any very great novels? It is kind of a Freudian organization of the Gothic materials. Now this leads to something which is quite bluntly a question. It would seem that the way Americans feel in a situation like this is either in terms of Freud or in terms of Puritanism, which they have overcome. Now, as in George Santayana's one novel, **The Last Puritan**, the Puritan who turns against Puritanism turns against it puritanically. That is to say, he gives up the context of the belief, so that the whole emotional soul is the thing. The dirty words, the shocking passages, the homosexual incidents described at some length would seem to me to be the result of a Puritan heritage.*

Uncle Al on *Pickwick Papers*

"Pickwick is a darb, Mike, he's a darb. He's a very civilized man, and he is interested in life. He's always going around the country to learn. He has great curiosity. And he has friends. One of them is named Winkle. Mike, he's one of these fellows who talks big and is never able to accomplish anything. He pretends he's a sportsman and he can't shoot a gun. And he can't skate. You know the type, Mike, one of these fellows who's all window and nothing in the store inside. I meet lots of them on the road, salesmen who talk in big figures, and you don't know how they earn their expense account. But Mike, you want to read this book, *Pickwick Papers*. Pickwick is a real gentleman, and he's always getting in trouble. He gets in the funniest jams all the time."

No Star is Lost

" . . . the beginning of the mystery of life is the mystery of ourselves."

What Is a Good Novel?

Excerpted from a draft of a lecture for delivery at the Textile
High School, New York City, February 16, 1950, to Fannia
Cohn's ILGWU girls

The way the experiences of others become interesting to us when
we read them in a novel, the way they seem to be worth our knowing
about, is this—we put ourselves in the place of the characters; as we
read, we identify ourselves with the characters. We see ourselves as
like them or not like them. In our imaginations we live with them, and
not simply with ourselves. In this way we get outside ourselves.

I want to stay on this point for a moment, because I believe that it is
very important. No matter who we are, no matter how much chance
we have to have a variety of experiences, no matter how much chance
we have to travel, to see things in life, there is a limitation upon what
we can do and what we can experience directly. Along with this, we
are all, in a sense, locked up in ourselves. We only know ourselves
well. We only know what goes on in our own minds and not what
goes on in the minds of others. We can know what goes on in the
minds of others only to the degree that they tell us what goes on in
their minds or to the degree that we can guess, on the basis of how
they act and what they say. This is very obvious but very important to
keep in mind—to keep in mind the fact that we can know only ourselves in an intimate way. How we tend, because of the nature of a human being, because of the simple and obvious fact that we can't know
others as we know ourselves, to see the world, always, in our own image. If we are gloomy, we are inclined to think that others are gloomy.
Whatever we are, whatever we seem to be to ourselves, that is what we
tend to see in other people.

Now, this suggests one of the most important values in what is often
called imagination. Imagination is capacity, in one way or another, to
guess at, to fancy, to think up that which we don't know for sure. One
interpretation of imagination is that which defines it as the thinking up
of what does not exist. But we can interpret imagination in another
way; we can also say that we mean by imagination the ability to guess,
the ability to put together, the ability to sense that which we do not
know for sure. If we think of imagination in these terms, and keep in
mind what I have just said concerning the simple and obvious fact that
we are locked up in ourselves and only know ourselves, we can get a

good idea of one of the very important things to be got out of reading novels—good novels, if I may say so. Whenever we read a novel that moves us very deeply, that absorbs and holds our attention, that keeps us thinking about the characters in the book, that leads us to want to know, very much, what happens to them, how they are going to come out at the end of the story, we get the feeling that we know the people in the book, these imaginary or fictional people, very well; that we know them better than we know our own friends, and ourselves. When we have this feeling, what we really do is to identify ourselves with these people. In a sense, we share the fate that the writer has given them in his books. We go through their sufferings. We hope when they hope. We want to see them achieve whatever they are moving toward, as though their ends might be our own. We laugh, we weep, we are sad and we are gay and happy in accordance with what happens to them in the story. We get outside ourselves. We get outside ourselves in the sense that we live with these other people; we live in their minds, we feel with them and not only with ourselves. This is a kind of an imaginary act. And when we do this, when we identify with the people in a book, we give ourselves the opportunity of understanding more, so that while we continue being locked up in ourselves, our own selves are no longer as narrow as they were. We have shared an imaginary experience with the characters created in a novel. And when we have shared this imaginary experience, we often find that we ourselves have confidence that we understand more, that we have a better sense of people, that we have a better sense of ourselves. We see that there are more possibilities in the ways in which we can feel about life, the ways in which we can look at life, than was the case before.

If we want to ask ourselves the question, What is a good novel? perhaps it is just as well to answer by saying that a good novel is, for us, a novel that permits us to have this kind of exprience, in which we share imaginatively in the feelings, the joys, the sorrows, the hopes and the tragedies of others about whom we read.

There is a difference between a daydream and the imagined story that we read in a good book. The patterns of daydreams are almost always the same. We imagine ourselves getting something that we want without cost. Even if we imagine ourselves doing what it is customary to do in order to get the thing we want—for instance, if we were a young boy and we imagined ourselves performing dangerous and heroic deeds in order to win the affections of a girl—even if we imagine this, there really is no cost to us. The danger is an empty danger that we invent. Usually, in a daydream, after inventing any danger we must go through in order to get what we want, we skip through that danger quickly and we achieve the end. There is a kind of monotony to day-dreaming. Daydreaming is not an experience in which we have many different emotions, in which there are many feelings involved in our minds. There is little danger of suffering, little danger of our becoming anxious—little danger of our having any troublesome emotions at all.

Now, when I say this I am not saying that we have to or should have anxious, troubled or sad emotions. I would say this: We just do have emotions of that kind. We just do not always see the world through rose-colored glasses. Part of living, part of developing, is to have sad as well as happy feelings, and to live through and to work through sad and unhappy and troublesome emotions and feelings. The daydream is an escape from these feelings. A good book, a novel that is real, that is sincere, is usually *not* an escape from these feelings but a facing of them. It tells us a story that, when we have read it, we say, Now, this is true, this is like life, this is like the way people act, or feel, or think, and this shows the way they face their own feelings and thoughts, or the way they face things in the world, or the way they face both them-selves and the world. We have something that is different from a day-dream.

Let us bring all of this together in the simple sentence, Life is a mys-tery. The world is a mystery. There are mysteries on all sides of us. And the beginning of the mystery of life is the mystery of ourselves. Along with the mystery of ourselves, there is the mystery of other people. We don't know ourselves too well, and we don't know other people very well. Novels in which there is some kind of truth help us to ex-plore the mystery, help to give us the feeling that life is a little less mys-terious, that life is a little less awesome and fearful.

So far, I haven't talked about certain aspects of novels that are stressed very much, that are talked about in criticism, in book reviews, in books about novels and about literature. That is style. That is writ-ing itself, the use of words. I am only going to make a few remarks about this side of novels and novel writing. I would begin by saying that words are used, or that we should see that words *can* be used, in two different ways. Words can be used to convey information. Sup-pose we say that a dress is black. When we say that a dress is black, the work "black" is used to convey information. Words are also used to convey emotions, to give some sense of the quality of a thing or an ex-perience and to capture something of that vague aura of feeling that surrounds everything we see. If, for instance, we are in a depressed or low mood, we might use the word "black" to describe it. When we say that we are in a black mood, we are not conveying information in the direct, precise, specific sense that we are when we say that a certain dress, which we know to be black, is black. In the first instance, we are using black in order to give information about some quality, something that can be seen. In the second instance, we are using the word black for an emotional reason. We are using the word to convey information, but not in as specific a sense as we are when we use it as the sign of a color. We are using it to convey or suggest a state of mind.

In our reading, it is well to remember this. We can then become less confused about style. Sometimes, a great deal of mystery is created about style and about good writing. Good writing is writing that is clear and that serves the purpose for which it is intended; if it is intended to give us information, it gives us that information without falsifying, in the best possible way, so that we can comprehend and understand it. Good writing, when it is intended to convey states of mind, makes clear the states of mind which the author intends to convey. So all that I would say here about style, and about writing, is that it should be as comprehensible as subject matter permits.

There are some subject matters that are more complicated than others. Also, in order for us to understand something, even if it is clear, we must have the ability to understand. We must have a certain amount of knowledge, a certain amount of experience in life. When I say knowledge, when I say experience in life, I do not mean this in a quantitative sense. I do not mean it as the number of facts that you know. And I do not mean it in the sense of the number of places you have been, necessarily. I mean it in the sense that whatever you have gone through, you know about, and that, in the course of living, you get to know something about people.

Let me explain my point this way. A child is, in most instances, likely not to understand a number of things that his father and mother say. Now, the father and mother may talk very clearly to each other. In this sense, the style of their talk is good. It serves its purpose. But the child is too young and has had too few experieces in life to permit it to understand some of the words of the father and mother. Now, the same is true in formal writing. In novels, in poetry, there are various styles and traditions of writing. In these styles, in these traditions, patterns of words, connotations of words, ways of using words develop. In some instances, a certain familiarity with these styles, with these traditions, is necessary before we are able to understand the work. Some books, then, require a certain amount of experience in reading before we can understand them very well. Now, there are two things about this. In some cases it is a matter of education and a matter of reading. In others it is a matter of our own experience. For instance, there are books that I now think that I can understand but that, when I was at the age of twenty-one, I could not understand as well. It is because of things like this that some people become bewildered and frightened about books. They become afraid that they will not understand, that they do not have enough education. This, however, is true of all of us. No matter how much we might think we know, we really know very little of all the knowledge that there is in the world, of all the knowledge that it is possible to acquire. It is the same with books and with art. Since the beginning of the history of man, some men have been creating art. They have been creating it in various forms—in pictures, in sounds, in words, in form. No one can know all of that art. No one can know all of those styles. You can know only some. It is best to try and find and know a little about those forms of art, those styles of art, that seem best suited to your needs, that seem to promise to give you a better sense of life, to permit you to enjoy life more and to understand more of it. We can say that good styles help with this, because good styles are like new eyes.

Let us look at it this way. Let us think of the world only as something we can see. Now, the possibilities of seeing objects, objects that will interest and please us in one way or another, are endless. We ourselves, in this world, tend to see very little of all that we may see. On the streets where we live, this is so. We often are unaware of the differing combinations of colors at different times of the day. We are unaware of how buildings look different in shadow, in sunlight, in twilight, when the colors of the day are changing. Suddenly, we might see a building across the street from us in just a different way, and it might suddenly interest us more, and we might even think it is beautiful, and in fully looking at it, we might have all sorts of vague wishes and images. Something might happen to us; we might become moody, excited, elevated. At times when we look at a picture, we see that an artist who has painted it has seen something differently from how we have seen it. At first we might look at it and think that it is impossible to see the way that the artist has seen. Then, as we continue to gaze at the picture, we gradually begin to see that the artist has loaned us his eyes, as it were, and we realize that we can see a little more in the world, a little more in this picture, than we could before.

It is the same with words—and this is something important about style. The way writers use words can be a kind of loaning of the brains and minds of writers to the reader. Just as, when we look at certain pictures, we get a sense of seeing more in the visual world, so, when we read, we sometimes may get an added sense of the use of words, which gives us the feeling and the conviction that we ourselves can better handle words, so that they serve us with those two purposes that are the primary purposes of words—to convey information and to create a sense of states of mind and an awareness of feelings and emotions.

That is all I care to say about style here. A good style helps to give us a new sense of words, new meanings for words, and permits us to use words in a way that helps us to understand more and to feel more. We can easily awe and bewilder ourselves if we turn the whole question of the use of words into a mystery.

Let me give you an example to clinch this point. When I was a student in high school, one night in a class the professor wrote two snatches of poetry on the board. He asked us to decide which we liked best. I recall that I was disturbed. I was afraid that I would choose the wrong verse. I would choose the one that was bad. Now, one of the verses was from Shakespeare. The other was a very banal, commonplace, sentimental, silly verse. I chose that one. Now, actually, I didn't know which one was better. I had become confused and was afraid that I would choose the wrong one. With something approaching desperation, I clutched at the verse that seemed the most familiar to me.

There are two things I want to say about this. One is that I did not, in that classroom, read both of those verses carefully and ask myself, Which of these verses means the most to me? I did not, in that moment, have an attitude such as the one I am trying to suggest here. I did not see my reading of those verses as something that would be of value to me. Rather, I saw it as a decision I would have to make that would meet with the approval or disapproval of someone outside of myself, someone who in a sense had authority over me. In addition, I was concerned with what my classmates would think after the teacher had told us which was the better of the verses. I was confused, and with that, I was not sincere. I did not look at those two snatches of verse in a way that they would have had any meaning for me in terms of my own development, my own feelings. I did not look at the words in them in the way I have tried to suggest in this talk. In part, at least, I tried to decide which of them was the best for the neighbors. The neighbors happened to be my classmates.

If we look at books in this way, we might just as well not read them. If we consider the question of what is a good book and what is a bad book in this context, it doesn't mean anything for us to like a book. When we can make books mean something to us, we are learning to live more, we are helping to develop ourselves, we are getting new ideas, new feelings and new understanding in our dealings with other people. We are learning about the use of words in such a way that we can live better through the words we use.

A second point I want to specify about my own experience is this—

that when we speak of good and bad books, we talk about taste. Taste is something we acquire. The beginnings of acquiring taste are to be found in reading whatever we read in a sincere way, just for ourselves and not for the neighbors. If we do that, we will find what is our own taste. In the last analysis, a good book to us is a book that is suited to our own taste. And I'll add that if our taste is for the neighbors, or to fool ourselves, it does not matter whether it comes from a good or a bad book, by any definition.

Abe Ginsberg's Taste in Fiction

"Mr. Saxon, do you really approve of that story?" lean, ascetic, Adam's-appled Abe Ginsberg asked.

"Well, Abe, that depends upon what you mean by approve."

"I want to know if you approve of it!" Abe repeated excitedly.

"Um...Considering that the author is a beginner, yes, I do. I believe that it shows promise. To the contrary, I don't approve of it in the sense that I would approve of a story by Poe, Kipling, O. Henry, Bret Harte, or Chekhov. Mr. Cogan is only starting out."

"You approve, then?"

"As I explained."

Abe smirked in arrogant derision, and the Professor asked O'Neill's opinion.

"I agree with Abe that it's lousy," said O'Neill, some of the girls tittering at his bluntness.

"But Abe didn't say precisely that."

"I do now!" Abe said, provoking added tittering.

From "The Professor,"
The Short Stories of
James T. Farrell

"Writing is meaningless unless the writer has complete sovereignty over his material."

Recent Developments in the Novel:
The Hero as Victim

Speech delivered at Wayne University in Detroit, February 12, 1954

Thank you. I spoke here about four years ago and I'm very glad to come back and talk to you again. Before talking about recent developments in novel writing, I want first to make a few remarks about the world we live in. We've had, perhaps, more revolutionary changes in our lifetime than in the entire history of the world. We are only nine years away from the bloodiest and most bitter war in history. Since 1945, we have lived in a period that has been characterized as a cold war, and it's neither war nor peace. We have lived in a state of continuing and constant international tension and crisis. We have had the discovery of the atom bomb, the unleashing of nuclear energy, and by and large all of us are more or less confused. We are trying better to locate ourselves on this planet.

The younger generation of writers has had a different kind of experience from that of writers of my age. You've heard much spoken about the 1920's, and it was most certainly an easier period for a writer to forge his own consciousness and gain a sense of his own aspirations, to struggle to find his own way of seeing things, than is the present. Writers of my generation were too young for one war and too old for another. The present generation of writers includes a number who spent some of the best years of their lives in war, in the army, regimented. We do not know how much this means in their lives and for their writing. We do not know whether it has been a good influence or a retarding influence. However, in the light of these facts, I think we should be careful not to take too harsh an attitude toward new American writers. They've come upon the scene and begun to write at a time when no one knows too much and anyone who is honest about it will admit that he does not know too much, and that there is definite reason for confusion and definite reason for concern and alarm.

I shall also say that, in this country at the present time, we have a dangerous situation due to a pressure for conformity and a recrudescence and resurgence of know-nothingism, where fear creates self-intimidation; this makes many people fearful and timid. I would here observe that we've also had a revival of efforts to censor books. Even books that have been read by hundreds of thousands of people are now again and again hauled into court, most dramatically, in the last year or two, in the city of Detroit.

With these general remarks in mind, I am going to speak first about a book that was published in Paris several years ago. It is entitled *The 25th Hour* and was written by a Rumanian emigre named Gheorghiu. It is the story of a Rumanian peasant who was caught up in the last war—in the waves of terrorism and totalitarianism and fighting that had spread across Europe. He is completely innocent but he is lugged from one to another German concentration camp. He is freed by the Americans and then put into a succession of *American* concentration camps. He is a man who has committed no crime, who has done no wrong, and yet who spends a great part of his life in a series of concentration camps, as a number and a slave, as a person with almost no identity. The author, Gheorghiu, organizes the book around the idea, or the hypothesis, that the real warfare of man is between man and the machine. Undoubtedly you know that Marxist philosophy had a considerable and widespread influence throughout Europe, and that it popularized the conception that there is a war of the classes at the roots of society; in *The 25th Hour* Gheorghiu substitutes for this idea the idea of war between man and machine. He says that the proletariat is the machine, and that it is going to enslave man. And he treats the concentration camp as a kind of machine.

The story is presented in a very rigid way. It opens with a realistic account of the chief protagonist on a farm in Rumania and then becomes fantastic, mechanical and arbitrary. The description of the American concentration camps is completely false, unrealistic and machinelike in its presentation. The Americans are described as though they were cogs in a machine terrorizing the central character. The book was very badly received in the United States but it was very well received in France. In passing, I'll say that in France, among writers and the intelligentsia, there is a great fear and disdain of machinery, and one of the criticisms that many French writers and intellectuals make of the United States is that it is a civilization of gadgets.

A distinguished, catholic and non-communist French literary figure and professor of philosophy, Gabriel Marcel, wrote an introduction to *The 25th Hour,* heralding it. If you had been in France at the time the book came out, you might have said, "Well, here is a new current in literature, here is something on which the future direction of liter-

97

ature will be predicated.'' Then, about two years after the book's publication, it was suddenly discovered—or was alleged, and there
seemed to be sufficient proof—that the author of this book had been
pro-Nazi; that he had been a Nazi agent. And a number of those critics
who had praised the book, and also Professor Marcel, who was an
honest and intelligent man, became alarmed; and Marcel and others
changed their minds and decided that *The 25th Hour* was not the
kind of book they had thought it was. My own opinion of the book is
that it is a very bad book, that it is a mad book, and that it is not of any
significance as a novel, although it is significant in terms of the reaction it evoked in France.

I tell this story because it cautions us against thinking we can predict trends in literature too easily. And it cautions us against thinking
that one book and its reception at a particular time necessarily predict
the future of the novel, necessarily demonstrate a tendency.

With this point in mind, let me recall to you the fact that since the
publication of the first novels of Ernest Hemingway, there has been a
whole series of interpretations of them. Back in the 1920's, Hemingway was described as the spokesman of a new and ''lost'' generation,
a generation that had been betrayed by the First World War, a generation that felt itself to be lost to the disillusionment that followed that
war. In the 1930's there was a new emphasis on the sociological approach to literature. There were a number of writers and critics who
attempted to analyze and interpret literature, including the novels of
Hemingway, in terms of Marxist thought; and there were a number
who did so with the interests of the Communist Party in mind, so that
they came to judge literature as social revelation, and often their
agreement with a writer's social philosophy was used as the key for
understanding and judging his books. Ernest Hemingway then became, instead of a spokesman of ''the lost generation,'' a decadent.
He became a man who did not believe in the future. He became a man
who believed in violence and death; and some people described him
practically as an unconscious, or a crypto- or a proto-fascist. Today
we have a different type of criticism. The New Critics look for symbolical meanings in all kinds of books, and Ernest Hemingway's
writing is now explored in the attempt to find in it symbols that will
justify the claim that Hemingway wrote and is writing myth and allegory.

Choose any writer and you will find, from generation to generation, the same kind of changes of attitude toward him. When something is discovered about his character, you will find sudden changes
of opinion.

Nevertheless, one tendency that has developed in contemporary novel writing is an emphasis on the purpose of literature as myth and allegory. Along with this, there has been a series of attacks on what is called realistic writing—sometimes the word "naturalism" is used. And if a writer is categorized as a realist or a naturalist rather than a writer who embodies myth and allegory in his work, he is considered to be inferior.

Now, I'll speak very briefly about naturalism.

If we say a book is realistic, we mean, most simply, that it assumes experience is grounded in reality. In distinction, naturalism was more or less founded by the French novelist Emile Zola. In 1878, he wrote an essay entitled *The Experimental Novel.* In it, Zola insisted that the purpose of the novelist was to become a scientist. He said that the time for personal impression in literature was gone, and that, just as the physiologist in his laboratory was a scientist, so was the novelist a scientist of human behavior. He said that the forces that shape human character were heredity and environment, and that the character of any human being was the consequence of the play of these forces upon him. He said that all romanticism was lies, and by lies he meant untruths. He made rigid and literal-minded associations between literature and the purposes of literature on the one hand and the ideas of the French scientists of the time, especially Claude Bernard, a physiologist, on the other. Zola denied the existence of free will; he adopted a definitely deterministic hypothesis.

In various fields, deterministic hypotheses are adopted; for instance, Freud was a determinist. But ever since Zola, any writer, whether he has read Zola or has not, whether he believes in free will or in determinism or says he doesn't know what he believes—even if he believes the question isn't an important one—still, if he can be classified as a realist or a naturalist, he can be and often is attacked because of the ideas that Zola expressed in the year 1878. A writer may not have read Zola or Zola's ideas on the novel, and he may not agree with them if he has read them. Nevertheless, inevitably and inescapably, Zola will be used as a whipping post and as a club to characterize and derogate him and any other writer who can be called a realist or a naturalist.

I mentioned that Zola described romanticism as untruths; but if one reads books of Zola's, such as *Nana,* the story of a glorified prostitute, a woman of the demi-monde and an actress, or *Germinal,* the story of a mine and a mine strike, which more or less refers to the founding of the First International, one will find that Zola himself was very romantic and symbolical in his way. His character Nana is symbolic of a "life force," of a destructive force—she's a symbol of what Zola believes to be the power of heredity. *Germinal* is full of the symbolism of light and darkness. The very title of the book, *Germinal,* is symbolic—so that Zola himself did not adhere to his notions of naturalism and his anti-romantic convictions.

Thus a novel is something very complex—and for this reason it is subject to more than one interpretation. A good novel cannot be considered and analyzed exhaustively in terms of one point of view. I make this point because I want now to refer to the notion that literature must deal with symbols and must deal with myths; that if a writer has a kind of vision, a way of seeing life, in which he looks at life directly and sees the meaning of experience in the experience itself, today he is inherently to be criticized and considered inferior by the various critics, called the New Critics, because he is not producing what they call myths and allegories.

One of the most influential writers of our time is Franz Kafka. Kafka lived with a German family in Prague, which is now Czechoslovakia, in the earlier years of this century. He was a man of extraordinary talent, probably a genius, almost certainly a great writer. He was also a seriously disturbed person—a person with a very weak ego. He wrote some remarkable books. When he died, I believe in the early 1920's, he wanted these books burned, but fortunately they weren't. One is called *The Trial.* Another is called *The Castle.* In *The Trial* and *The Castle,* the chief protagonist does not even have a name. He is referred to as Mr. K. In *The Trial,* Mr. K. is to be put on trial, but he does not know what he is to be tried for. He cannot find the court. In *The Castle,* Mr. K. is an engineer who travels to a certain town in Germany, where he is supposed to go to a castle and there be told what to do. Mr. K. can never get there; he gets entrapped and lost on the winding roads that lead to it.

You might say that these books are written from the standpoint of a dream, an hallucination. You might say that what Kafka does is to make an hallucination seem immediate and real. His method of presentation is quite similiar to that of certain contemporary writers who are called realists, in that everything is presented from the standpoint of immediate experience. Kafka presents everything that happens as though it were happening before our eyes, and his selection and organization of details is governed by what has direct bearing on his character in a particular situation. There is something frightening to many people and bewildering and disturbing to almost everyone in Kafka's writing. All of the ordinary premises that we assume, as though they were part of ourselves and part of the order of life and being—these are in effect challenged. Status, place, home, name—all of these things are challenged. Kafka's characters do not possess the ordinary minimum of identification that distinguishes each of us from another and that allows us to know who we are, where we are, where we live, what our status is.

Kafka himself, as I said, was a disturbed man. If psychiatrists analyzed and made deductions about the personality of Kafka from the records—from his diaries, from letters and from his books—I believe they would find it plausible to say that he was probably psychotic. In some of his little fables and stories he introduces the character as a mole or as a mouse. I mean that there is a reduction of the ego in his work. Now this disturbance in Kafka's characters is quite genuine. Kafka took his own need for security as the basis for exploring and revealing his experience; he used his own emotional life as the material for literature. In doing so, he exhibited a sort of drive for normality, a kind of a drive to escape from the sense of a lack of identity. In addition, since his characters are as though entrapped in a kind of spiritualized bureaucracy, Kafka has often been described, and I think with justice, as having had a prophetic insight into the nature of the world in which we live—a world in which what we consider to be individuality is threatened, and seriously threatened.

Kafka has had an influence all over the world, and he has become an influence upon many writers of the younger generation in this country. I will briefly take one novel in which his influence can be felt. It did not receive a great deal of attention when it was published and possibly is now forgotten, but it will permit me to make a point, I believe, briefly and concretely. The novel is *The Bitter Box,* by Eleanor Clark. It is the story of a bank clerk. The bitter box is the little cage in which the bank clerk works. The bank clerk is a man of no particular character, no outstanding trait of personality. He works as though he were a prisoner in his cashier's cage. In some curious way he becomes involved with Communists and entrapped. And in the end, as I recall the novel, he is merely confused.

Now there is a difference between this novel and Kafka's own writings, his own sickness; where Kafka takes direct hold of his own disturbed experience, this book is a kind of a screen between the author and the reader. It is very cold. It is almost meaningless.

I mention all of this for this reason: One of the few countries in the world where there has been a normality and continuity of experience, where there hasn't been foreign invasion or sharp and disruptive social change, is the United States. I began this lecture by mentioning Gheorghiu; much has been said about the French Existentialist

101

writer Jean-Paul Sartre. One of Sartre's ideas, or one of his claims, is that the literature of today must be a literature in which extreme situations are treated; and in significant or influential works that have come from Europe—in books like *The 25th Hour*—an extreme situation *is* presented, a situation that is the consequence of a profound and shaking, all-encompassing capacity, in the same sense that Kafka's work is a work that deals with extreme situations.

Now, in the United States, even though we've had the bitterest war in history, there has been a kind of continuity of life; there has been and still is an opportunity for many people of a new generation. We have not suffered the extreme crises that France and Germany and even England have, and I think this goes far to explain why the influence of Kafka often seems unreal in the United States. And it seems to me that, in the same way, the novel that treats myth and allegory, the novel with an emphasis on symbolism, just doesn't seem true, or representative, or believable here.

You know, the German philosopher Hegel, in his book *Esthetics,* said that allegory was an inferior form of writing because it is cold, it is feelingless. Well, that may or may not be true in all cases. It is not true in the case of Kafka, because his work comes so intimately out of his own way of seeing and out of his own experience. It does seem to be true of the writings of those who have attempted to imitate Kafka; who have attempted, more or less consciously, to concoct or invent symbols, myths, and fables in furtherance of the notion that this is the only way in which one ought to write.

I'd like to make a second observation about some newer writing, keeping in mind, as I said earlier, that we should take a somewhat patient and charitable attitude toward newer work because of the greater confusion in the world. One thing I have observed in some of the younger writers I have read is an increasing tendency to present the neurotic victim as a hero and to present an image of the world in terms of the neurotic victim's vision.

For purposes of illustration, I'm going to take a bad book. The book I'm going to take is *Knock on any Door* by Willard Motley. The sense of *Knock on any Door* is that if you knock on any door, behind it you'll find a homicidal maniac who has been created by society. The novel is the story of an Italian boy, an altar boy, who is treated brutally and becomes delinquent; from a delinquent, he becomes a jackroller, a robber, a cop hater and a murderer. Finally he is executed. The book is organized quite like an ordinary, representative Hollywood movie. You've seen them—the kind in which the boy meets the girl.

Think of this: Suppose some intelligent being from Mars were to come and see one of those movies, and on the basis of the movie were to attempt to describe the society that produced it. He might make a series of deductions like this: Here is a society that is rich, where there is great versatility and cleverness, where all kinds of products are put out, where there is a high level of comfort, where most people have automobiles that go fast, and so on. And it would seem that one of the main things that this society does is to put all this effort into the task of helping a boy get a girl when he doesn't know how to get her without help.

I remember there was a picture I saw some years ago that illustrates this. It was called *Gilda*. The hero's name, incidentally, was Johnny Farrell. I'm glad that his name wasn't James. This character, Johnny, was very passive. Gilda, I believe, was played by Rita Hayworth. And one of the characters was a gents'-room philosopher who talked with an Italian accent. He had one function in the picture—his function was to tell Johnny that Rita loved him when he didn't know it. He finally convinces Johnny of this and helps to create the situation at the end of the picture wherein Johnny can stand and put his arms out like this and say, "Take me."

There are any number of pictures like this. The incidental characters in them are related to the boy and the girl. Unless there are special reasons, no other girl can be better dressed or more beautiful. The other characters cannot have more lines. Their lines must have bearing on the boy and the girl and on getting them together. In other words, there is a series of hierarchies determining how much space, what kind of lines, and so on, the various characters have; and they are all based on the relationship of elements to these two central characters. And in the same way, but negatively, *Knock on any Door* is organized.

The author of *Knock on any Door* has a generalized idea of social responsibility. He doesn't motivate it. The incidental characters are given large parts and detailed treatment in direct proportion to their sympathy for the boy who becomes delinquent; they are treated well or badly by the the author according to what attitude they take toward the boy. The author doesn't show clearly how and why society is responsible for the boy's downfall; he asserts it.

In the questioning, if some of you will ask me about *An American Tragedy,* I will give a counteranalysis to show how I think a writer can really present a case of societal responsibility in a book, but I won't take the time to do that now. I'll continue: The author of *Knock on any Door* has a generalized conception that society has

103

made this boy what he is, and the boy is merely a passive consequence of the ill treatment he receives. At the end of the book, when
the boy is waiting to be electrocuted, a social worker, who represents
the author's point of view, writes the boy a letter and says, You were
not guilty; you did nothing. Now murder, even of a policeman, is not
nothing. It is something. And this attempt to absolve a character of all
responsibility for his actions—not to trace a pattern of guilt, not to
trace to the end the psychological consequences of an action—this is
bound up with what I mean when I say there is a tendency in the
newer writing to present the neurotic victim as a hero, to present an
image of society in terms of its relationship to the neurotic victim.

There are better examples of this. For instance, there is a writer in
Chicago, not of the younger generation but not, I believe, much over
forty, who is a writer of extraordinary power—Nelson Algren. Algren
writes about what sociologists would call marginal groups, groups
that do not have a clear social status—dope fiends, people who live in
flop houses and in cheap hotels, delinquent boys and prostitutes.
Now Algren shows an intense and deep sympathy with these people;
and there is insight, and there are flashes of power, and there is at
times a very strong poetic feeling in his work. But in the two of his
novels I have read, *Somebody in Boots* and *Never Come Morning,*
there is not a sustained underlying structure or exploration of the
emotions involved in the story. Particularly in *Never Come Morning,*
there is a tendency by Algren to paste on to the action of the book, or
to imbue his characters with, a kind of disturbed and sick feeling that
certain sensitive or oversensitive writers possess. And this is what I
mean by saying that one tendency in contemporary novel-writing,
then, is toward a kind of projection that itself tends to celebrate the
victim as the hero.

In order to make this clearer I'll allude briefly to the French writer
Gustave Flaubert. I'm certain that if a psychiatrist were to examine the
records of Flaubert, he would say that Flaubert was neurotic, that he
was "obsessive-compulsive" that he had a homosexual complex, and
more, and there might be some justification for saying so. Flaubert
was very obsessive, he wasn't strongly attracted to women, and so
on; but if you take the writing of Flaubert, and particularly if you take
one of his great books, *Madame Bovary*—the story of a bored wife in
a French provincial town, Rouen, who has a love affair that leads to
her destruction; she goes into this love affair out of an impulse for
experience that will be romantic and ideal—you will see that Flaubert
was fighting within himself his own tendencies toward romanticism.
In fact, he described himself as Madame Bovary; when asked, he said,

"Madame Bovary . . . it is I." Now I mention *Madame Bovary* for this reason: In the case of Flaubert, a writer about whom you could make an argument that in his personal life he was neurotic, you do not get the same kind of a presentation or created image of the world that you do in a book such as *Knock on any Door.* Rather you get a writer who is struggling with himself, who takes his own tensions and struggles and makes of them material—not only for him to come to some terms with himself and to crystallize his own experience, but out of that to make a clearer, and if the word means anything, a more normal vision of the world.

Let us return briefly to Gheorghiu, to *The 25th Hour,* a book that shows a deep and a fundamental insecurity. The central character himself is insecure. The central character himself loses his freedom of movement and is a victim. In this case, and in the case of Kafka, whom I admire, and of *Knock on any Door,* which I don't, there is this same passivity. Now, as I said at the beginning of this lecture, we live in a world in which there are many dangers and much confusion; we have come to a turning point in history, have entered a new age, the atomic age; and there are grounds for a sense of insecurity, for many of us to feel unsure of ourselves. And I think that this uncertainty has come most definitely into European and American fiction, good and bad—that is, books that I consider good and bad; books that, in my opinion, are of some significance and value, and perhaps will be of lasting significance, and books that will quickly be forgotten. Now I'm not going to say that this shouldn't be, I'm not going to say that writers should write differently. I feel that writing is meaningless unless the writer has complete sovereignty over his material. If he wishes to choose the victim as a subject and if his feeling is one of attraction to the victim, well, then, he should write that way. I merely make this observation: that one of the significant tendencies or one of the significant changes in writing today, as in the writing of an older generation of American writers, like Sinclair Lewis and Theodore Dreiser, and as in the writings of a great number of the masterpieces of the nineteenth century—one of the changes is that there is a growing feeling of insecurity, and there is the creation of a new type of hero. The new type of hero is the victim.

"We have a new world in which we understand very little. . ."

The Writer and His Audience

Speech delivered at the State Teachers College in Indiana,
Pennsylvania, June 12, 1958.
Speaker of the introduction is unknown.

Mr. James Farrell is a Chicago-born writer and lecturer who studied at the University of Chicago and has held various jobs—as a clerk, salesman and reporter—and has spent many anxious and enjoyable hours hitchhiking his way around the country. Chicago's south side and Chicago's working people were the basis for most of his writing, and literary influences include the famous American naturalist Theodore Dreiser, the Irish poet and author James Joyce and the French author Marcel Proust. Mr. Farrell's first work of prominence was a triology of novels dealing with the life of Studs Lonigan. The first of these books, Young Lonigan, *is a realistic novel with a stream-of-consciousness treatment of an adolescent growing up in the squalid south side of Chicago.* The Young Manhood of Studs Lonigan *is the second in the series and deals with Lonigan's adult life and his entanglement in the Chicago underworld. This brings about the decay of his soul, if he can be said to have a soul. The final novel,* Judgment Day, *shows the defeat and death of Studs Lonigan. The second hero on the American scene that Mr. Farrell has created is Danny O'Neill, another Chicago boy, whose life was last treated in a 1953 novel,* The Face of Time. *Again the technique is naturalistic but the philosophy is slightly more hopeful.*

Mr. Farrell has written many short stories and essays, dealing both with American and European life. He has traveled extensively in the United States and Europe, recently touring many of Europe's capitals and acquainting himself with the social and economic problems there. Most recently he has published two articles, one in The Nation *and one in* Coronet, *the former dealing with baseball as a business and revealing some of the enthusiasm Mr. Farrell has always felt for baseball; the latter dealing with adolescent problems in the United States.*

Today Mr. Farrell is to speak on the writer and his audience.

Thank you very much. I'm not going to speak personally about the writer and his audience. I'm going to make some remarks and observations which, perhaps, will help us to gain some general perspective on the subject. It's a line of thinking that I have been following for the last few years—and one in which I'm still engaged. I must read more and observe more before I can finally publish these ideas.

When I came here today, I stopped in the railroad station and looked at the newsstands. I looked at the reading material on the newsstands. There were pictures of girls—not as fresh looking or as good looking as the girls here, but, anyway, girls. And there were *True Confessions* and *Real Confessions*, and there were various kinds of romances that were shameful and shocking and so on. The reprint books looked equally bad; I mean that they looked like cheesy murder stories and commonplace he-man tales. The newspapers didn't look very good, either. In fact, the only reading material that a normally intelligent human being could have bought were two books. One was an old book of the newspaper reporter, John Guenther. The other was a novel called *Company K*, a novel of the First World War by William March. If you travel and go to hotels, you find it worse. Now, in the railroad stations and hotels one does not usually find the so-called bottom or most depressed people of American society. To a considerable extent you find men on expense accounts; you find executives, both senior executives and junior executives who don't become senior executives until they go to psychoanalysts to *become* senior executives, and you find young doctors like my brother who makes a fortune because he's a psychoanalyst and tells these men how to get ahead. You find leaders of American society.

I wonder, who is it who wants this junk? Is it these men? Is it the people who put it out, or is it a number of men who are the beneficiaries and also the solid backbone, the conservative backbone, of American society? I don't know who wants it; but if you travel around and look at this junk, there is reason to ponder and there is reason to speculate about it.

With this in mind, I would like to speak of a book that was published in the year 1867. It's a great American novel, and one that would have had an important and perhaps a profound influence on American writing if anybody knew about it. The book is *Miss Ravenel's Conversion from Secession to Loyalty*, by John William De Forest. It's a novel about the Civil War; the scenes are laid in a New England town, New Haven, really, and in New Orleans at the time of Gen. Ben Butler, who was the Yankee general in command of the city.

On the one hand, De Forest felt that the Puritan vein in New England had become very thin and narrow; that a kind of a frost had come upon the soul or spirit or mind of New Englanders. He contrasted this with the sense of warmth in the South. At the same time, he had a democratic, pro-Northern point of view, and showed it in contrasting the attitudes and ideas that distinguished North from South. He wrote very realistically about war. In a college edition of *Miss Ravenel's Conversion*, the editor, whose name, unfortunately, I forget, made parallel selections of De Forest's descriptions of war and the agony of battle and of Stephen Crane's in *The Red Badge of Courage*. De Forest's writing seems more vivid, even, than Crane's. Furthermore, De Forest provided a more realistic treatment of women. There was less gushing, and there was even an indication of an affair out of wedlock. This was described with taste, but there it was.

Now, at that time, the main group of readers in America was women, and young women, and they were used to romance; they were used to stories of the blue and the gray, stories of the heroics of battle. That time, I might say in passing, was the time when we had the beginning of the creation, particularly in the North, of the myths of Southern culture. While the North, having won the Civil War, was literally raping the South, it was writing novels about Southern culture. In those circumstances, William De Forest's novel was just impossible; it was practically ignored because there was no audience for it. The audience that existed would not stand for, would not be interested in, a novel that was more realistic than what it was accustomed to, that had some insight into the nature of characters and events and the nature of human experience. I am of the opinion that this book is almost as great a novel as *War and Peace*, but it has only been discovered recently; it was only discovered because an audience had been found for it. Before a book like this can exert an influence, before it can be received and studied in colleges, an audience has to be created. From generation to generation the audience for books differs.

With those remarks in mind, I will make a contrast between the United States and France. Perhaps the greatest literary tradition in modern times is that of France. There are so many great books in France that a Frenchman can spend his whole life reading French literature and still not have read all of the great books. When the novel developed in France, there was already a very highly developed culture; there was already a, perhaps not corrupt but extremely sophisticated and well-educated upper class, or aristocracy. There was a middle class that was challenging the aristocracy, which also numbered many intelligent and alert people. There were the Encyclopedists and before them men like Descartes and Leibnitz. There were great writers who were aristocrats and great writers who were bourgeois, and so on. The French novel began with a very high level of awareness.

I think, offhand, of three of the earlier French novels. One is *La Princesse de Cleves* (1678) by Madam La Fayette, who was a friend and possibly the mistress of La Rochefoucauld. It is the story of a virtuous woman. But in the treatment of amorous relationships, the understanding which the characters have of their own emotions is quite extraordinary. The second is a book called *Le Liaisons Dangereuses*, or *Dangerous Acquaintances*, by Choderlos de Laclos, which was written in the 1880's. Although little known in the United States, it's classic for its purity of style and for its many characters; but again I stress that there was this awareness of what was being done, awareness of human emotions. The same can be said of another novel, *Adolphe* (1815), by Benjamin Constant de Rebecque. In all of these three books, I will repeat, the characters understand a great deal about their own emotions. There is a high level of sophistication, of sophistication in a good sense, and there was an audience that could understand it.

Contrast that with early American literature of pioneer country, a country to which the major portion of immigrants who came were the rejected, the disinherited of the earth. Many of them did not speak the common language, English. Some of the earlier among them were indentured servants. Some of the earlier Irish were on a level of literacy a little bit above that of the Arabs of the present time. Some of them practically lived in caves. If we think of this, we can understand how there were crude and primitive beginnings of American writing—and that is true except in New England.

Let me return to *Miss Ravenel's Conversion*, which, I emphasized, was published in 1867. The cultural consequences of the Civil War were to a considerable extent to shift some of the geographical centers of American culture. We know that one of the sources of American culture and writing was the frontier, which was quite distinct from New England. The American historian Frederick Jackson Turner, in one essay in the 1890's, opened a new perspective on the great role of the frontier in shaping American democracy. While his ideas may not be completely sound, they did afford us new and rich insights into the nature of American experience. We know that American prose style was largely changed, was loosened up, by Mark Twain, and that Mark Twain depended on the frontier humorists and newspapers and so on. This has been well documented by researchers and by such others as the late Bernard De Voto. In that period there was also a growth of science; there were the beginnings of an interest in Darwinism. In 1876 Johns Hopkins University was founded. It was interesting—

when Johns Hopkins University was founded, Thomas Henry Huxley was invited to deliver the opening address. Those of you who are students of English literature will know of the controversy in education between Huxley, who was a biologist and evolutionist, and, say, Cardinal Newman. I mention these things in particular, but a number of things were happening in America, in science, sociologically, politically. There were new streams of immigrants arriving. And out of those things we had the basis of changes in American writing and of changes in the consciousness of people which led to a different kind of audience from the kind that De Forest encountered.

In this connection, Theodore Dreiser is of considerable importance. Theodore Dreiser's importance is not necessarily that he was, or is called, a naturalist. The term "naturalist" is often misused; it is often used merely as a category. Theodore Dreiser is important because he is one of the first modern American writers who attempted to come to terms with the character of American experience. And there are some interesting things about Dreiser that have been largely unrecognized by a number of critics and literary historians. One is this: Dreiser's father was a German immigrant; he came from the Rhinish country and he was quite rigid in his religious views. He spoke German. The first school that Dreiser went to was a German-American parochial school, where his classes were taught in German. Dreiser has apparently given a portrait of his father which is not completely fair. In his less pious moments, his less worried moments, the father used to sing songs to the Dreiser children—he sang them in German. Now I mention this because Dreiser's style, which often is loose, careless, has a Germanic quality and is related to his early experience. His early experience grows out of the immigration of his father—the coming of the immigrants to America—and we haven't studied enough the effects of this immigration. We haven't realized fully the extent to which the coming of waves of immigrants from many countries affected not only those who came and the first generation born here, but the first two and three generations after that. They affected the character of American thinking and feeling and of American writing to degrees unknown, and there is much here for us to understand and to reassess in considering American writing.

I think it is important to view, in relationship to this, awareness. It was impossible for us to have a developed awareness, a developed consciousness of self, such as the French had, because we didn't have stabilized classes, a stabilized culture or even a stabilized language. To a considerable degree the French language has been fixed for well over a century, whereas the American language is changing every day. *Studs*

Lonigan was mentioned earlier; well, many of the words of *Studs Lonigan*, which were common slang at the time, are no longer used. In 1919, if I can skip ahead, H. L. Mencken published the first edition of *The American Language*, in which he argued, whether correctly or not, that there is a distinct American language, which is different from the English language. Whether or not you agree with that, you will probably agree that the American language is, at least, a clear variation from the English language. Into it have gone all kinds of words from many languages; it has even been influenced by the Chinese, and Chinese words have come into it.

Now, to come back to Dreiser: Dreiser's first novel was written in 1899 and published in 1900—*Sister Carrie*. That was the beginning of the period of the decline of the small town and the triumph of the city. There is an interesting book by a professor in the Middle West—I believe his name is Anderson—published by the University of Pennsylvania, called *Main Street and The Middle Border*, in which the decline of the midwestern town, and its relation to the coming of the railroads, and later the automobile, and to the development of the national trade brand—in other words, to the expansion of American business and consumer industries—is shown.

In 1900 in Chicago there was a kind of easy night life, with actors and saloon keepers and salesmen and the like, and it was connected with the sports world and the theater. Chicago was smaller than New York. A man like *Sister Carrie's* George Hurstwood, who was the manager of an elegant saloon and restaurant, was a very big character in Chicago, whereas in New York he would be of little consequence. Dreiser was aware of that; he even states it. Sister Carrie goes off with Hurstwood, who is married. Out of some warmth and capacity of her nature she rises in the world and becomes an actress, and Hurstwood goes into a decline. As a matter of fact, the decline of Hurstwood is one of the gripping and tragic characterizations in American literature. I remember that my old English teacher, the late James Weber Linn, said that reading of Hurstwood was like watching a man slowly sliding down an icy precipice, and grabbing and grabbing until he has slid to total doom.

The publisher, Doubleday, Page and Company, and the publisher's wife were quite shocked by *Sister Carrie*, because it was a case in which the wages of sin were not death.

Another American writer, whom I would recommend as having been a very important influence in American writing and a better writer than is recognized, was Frank Norris. Frank Norris was a reader at Doubleday, Page and he recognized Dreiser—recognized Dreiser's superiority to himself, as a matter of fact—and more or less snuck out, or sent out half sub-rosa, review copies of *Sister Carrie*, which were being held. The reception of the book was mixed. On the one hand there were those who denounced it, called it evil and claimed that Dreiser was a menace to the Republic—although, in passing, the Republic, shaky as it may be, still stands in spite of *Sister Carrie*. A few reviewers recognized Dreiser. But the publisher and his wife sabotaged the book; apparently they just put it in a cellar and refused to sell it. It was published in England, and five years later, according to the story, the English novelist, Arnold Bennett, came to the United States on a visit. He was met by ship reporters and was asked what American he wanted to meet, and he said, Theodore Dreiser. Most of the ship reporters didn't know who the hell Theodore Dreiser was. And that was one of the ways America came to recognize that it had a major modern novelist.

The attitudes about what could or could not go into a book; attitudes about content; attitudes about the moral character of literature were such that *Sister Carrie* was largely unacceptable in 1900. That fact stands in striking contrast to the facts of the reception of a novel Dreiser wrote when he was over fifty, a novel that was his first popular success—*An American Tragedy*. I'm going to skip from 1900 to 1925, the period of *An American Tragedy*, for a very important reason, or at least I think it is an important reason. It is this—that there was a sharp change in American culture at the end of the First World War. When the United States entered the First World War it was a debtor nation; it emerged a victor, a creditor nation and, in spite of what is said about U.S. isolationism and the League of Nations, a major power in the affairs of the world. It had had new contact with Europe. The major capital investments for the development of American industry had been made by that time, and the railroads had been laid. By 1883 or thereabouts, America had already become the world's major producer of industrial goods. The preconditions of what we will call a consumer-oriented economy—wealth and productivity and a large, skilled labor force—had been established. In the 1920's we can see the results of this. There was an increase of investment in various types of consumer goods, and there was an increase of investment in culture; we also have the beginnings of the linking up—there is some falsity in it, but it is commonly accepted now—of entertainment and culture. There arose new publishing houses and new styles, not only in books but in the jackets and the manufacture of books. As a matter of fact, the publisher Alfred A. Knopf is largely responsible for making books more attractive than they had been. The Book of the Month Club was established, and you have the beginnings of the Theater Guild. You have new, popular, mass-circulation magazines like *Time* and *Life*—or rather like *Time; Life* came later. You have new money flowing into the motion-picture industry and a rapid expansion of it; and an impetus is given to the development of the motion-picture actor and actress— the star, a new kind of American royalty. In 1920 radio was introduced commercially; by the end of the 1920's it was a major industry. And so on—night clubs, and service and entertainment and cultural products of all kinds, including literature and the book business, expanded enormously.

At the same time there were the beginnings of a change of emphasis in American writing. If you take some of the serious and even some of the more popular writing of the 1920's, you can see that characters are treated more often in the roles they take in their leisure time. Characters are treated as consumers. Consider, say, Ring Lardner, who was, I think, one of the outstanding American writers of this century, and ask yourself what kinds of work his characters do; practically every one of them who works is concerned with leisure and entertainment. Or take the world of Ernest Hemingway; except for a few stories of boyhood and one or two stories about prize fighters, it's a tourist's world of Americans abroad. In the same way, Scott Fitzgerald's is a world of young people finding and adjusting themselves in the so-called Jazz Age. They corresponded to a new generation coming into economic and social maturity in an American way of life that was changing.

To some degree, we can see this reflected in Dreiser's *An American Tragedy. An American Tragedy* is based upon a famous murder case that happened in upstate New York, near Saranac Lake, in 1908—the Chester Gillette–Grace Brown murder case. The character Clyde Griffith, in whom Dreiser put much of himself, his own youth, lives a peculiar boyhood life. When the novel opens, Clyde is a boy, and his parents are itinerant, street-corner religious peddlars, preaching salvation in San Francisco as the crowds come home from work. As I recall, Dreiser says that they were attempting to dent the apathy of life. The boy, Clyde, is more or less embarrassed by them. He's more bewildered than embarrassed; I mean, his is not a normal boy's life. He moves from city to city. He doesn't have a fixed residence, a fixed school, fixed associations and so on. This first experience with life, this first education in life, more or less corresponds with Dreiser's own, because Dreiser was educated in life much more than he was in universities or school. Clyde became a bellboy in a hotel. Now, we can say that there is almost a hotel subculture in America. In a hotel—and the best ones are like palaces—a poet is indistinguishable from a sales-man or a politician or a gangster, and he is even respected by them if he can pay the bill. There are men on expense accounts, away from home, and they have certain kinds of impulses and inclinations; and there are many who consider themselves self-made, and they don't have much taste in how they spend the boss's money. And so on. This was Clyde Griffith's first experience with life and with how the rich live, but it was not really with the rich, in the sense of an established social class. There were the rich who had come out of the vast melting pot that we call America. With no means of judging, Clyde Griffith ab-sorbs from them the standard, as he sees it, of the good life.

In the earlier Dreiser writings we have dramas of success and failure, grandeur and misery. We have the character Cowperwood, a financer in the trilogy *The Titan* and *The Financer* and *The Stoic,* which was begun in 1910 or 1911 but was not finished until shortly before Dreiser's death. Cowperwood, who in psychological terms is, perhaps, one of the most mature characters created in modern Ameri-can literature, is a financial genius and a wizard. There are several other of Dreiser's characters who are material successes in the world, in that they achieve something or get some place, climb higher on the social or economic ladder. One is Sister Carrie. Another is Eugene Witla of the novel *The Genius,* published in 1916. It is a novel that I think has more to it than critics recognize and that still is worth read-ing. Witla has talent, sensibility, capacity and drive. Whether you con-sider these characters moral or immoral, socially useful or socially harmful, they succeed on their own.

But Clyde Griffith's concept of success—or his notion of success, because he does not have a concept—is of success by affiliation. In contrast to the treatment of wealth in the earlier books of Dreiser, in *An American Tragedy* the emphasis is on how it is enjoyed, not on how it is created or made. Grown, Clyde sets out to murder Roberta Alden, a factory girl who has become pregnant by him, so that he can marry a rich girl, Sandra Finchley. At the last minute, in the lake—he has taken Roberta rowing—the boat turns over and he loses his nerve; he doesn't technically kill her, but he allows her to drown and he is im-mediately caught.

Until this moment society has been virtually unaware of Clyde Grif-fith. He has lived on the fringes of a socially normal life. But from then and there, all of the force and energy of society is devoted to ferreting out and bringing to light practically every detail of Clyde Griffith's life—for the purposes of the court trial, for purposes of newspaper sensation; in order to see him, his mother even gets an assignment to

write about the case. He goes to the electric chair and he goes peni-
tent; and it's a penitence that is realized for a guilt that is emotionally
felt. It is not a false or phony guilt that Griffith feels. My point is, however, that the minute Clyde Griffith becomes an object for others, society then takes notice of him; there is no amount of money, or time,
or energy that cannot be spent upon him. This reflects and registers
the kind of change I have suggested—the change to an emphasis on a
life of leisure and consumption, even to the point of turning the human tragedy that happens in *An American Tragedy* into an object of
sensation, in order to produce a kind of writing that is parallel to the
writing I described in the magazines and books on the railroad-station
newsstands in Johnstown.

Now today, we skip from there to the present, but before we do it I
would like to mention this. We spoke of awareness—of a high level of
awareness in the development of the French novel and of a more
primitive level of awareness in the beginnings of American literature.
This is for understandable reasons, which I have suggested: the heterogeneous, polyglot character of America, the fact that it was not a fixed
and stable country, the fact that people of so many different levels of
experience came here and that they all were equal, and so on. And, of
course, if you have read about early conditions of American education, you are aware that they were crude. A book worth reading in this
connection—a significant and interesting document although not a
great book—is *The Hoosier Schoolmaster* by Edward Eggleston,
describing among other things conditions of education in the 1880's
in Indiana, at the time when Dreiser was growing up, as a matter of
fact—at the time of his early boyhood. This is understandable.

I have mentioned briefly the decline of the small town, the coming
of the railroad, the automobile and the national trade brand. In the
1890's there was the development of the mass-circulation magazine,
particularly *The Saturday Evening Post*. An early editor of *The Saturday Evening Post* was Edward Bok, and the autobiography of Edward
Bok is an extraordinary American document. Bok was an immigrant.
After Bok, George H. Lorimer developed *The Saturday Evening Post,*
and Lorimer wrote a book called *Letters of a Self-Made Merchant to
His Son.* Those two books were really important in the development
of the American idea of success and of American commercial culture,
because, with the development of the mass-circulation magazine and
newspaper, we had the beginnings of the real commercialization of
American culture. In magazines like *The Saturday Evening Post*—although they published some very important stories, particularly of
Ring Lardner; Ring Lardner's extraordinary and perhaps great novel

115

You Know Me Al, a novel that describes baseball as it may never again be described, first appeared in *The Saturday Evening Post*—the purpose of most of the writing was to sell goods. The advertising interests dominated, and by and large people were not permitted to be troubled by what they read in the pages of the magazine, because that creates bad will. In passing, there was a mediocre novel published in 1911, called *It Pays to Advertise.* Offhand, I forget the name of the author, but the novel was an illustration of how to make money by advertising. With mass-circulation magazines and national trade-brand products, advertising became an influence in American culture, and in the 1920's it became a more important influence, particularly through radio.

With new means of communication—not only mass-circulation magazines but movies—something else happened: When you make such a large investment and have to have such a heterogeneous audience to sustain it, it is dangerous to offend anybody. The larger a business is, the more it needs to create good will in the consumer market—so that, as you may have noticed, there are almost no movies in which a villain has a definite social status and occupation. A dead man makes a good villain, because there is no Association of Dead Men to protect the dignity of the dead. Villainy is good publicity for gangsters and they don't care much about their respectability, anyway, so gangsters are good villains. A Communist is a good villain for obvious reasons. It's very difficult, however, to find other kinds of villains, because if a villain is a lawyer, the lawyers will raise hell; if a villain is a grocer or an undertaker the grocers' and undertakers' associations will protest. The trade associations and professional associations are so jealous of the dignity of the occupations and professions they represent that it is quite dangerous for a mass-circulation medium, like motion pictures or television, to have a villain with an occupation. An amusing instance of this problem took place in the 1920's. The hotel owners of Atlantic City sent an appeal to the motion picture studios in which they asked that when businessmen in motion pictures go on fictional weekend vacations to Atlantic City they please take their wives instead of their secretaries, because Atlantic City was getting a bad name.

Now, a kind of pressure was brought to bear on American culture, and it was brought to bear most directly on those cultural industries, those cultural endeavors, that had the largest audiences. We find that a kind of fruition of this tendency has been reached with television, because television is almost completely dependent upon the advertiser for revenues. The purpose of a television program has nothing to do with giving us insight into experience, with making us more conscious, which in turn helps us to gain a sense of identity based upon some reality about life, characters and events. This is what serious literature and serious culture do. Television is concerned with selling goods, and, more and more, recently, with selling goods that we don't necessarily need. It is now concerned with selling a new refrigerator when an old one would do. It is concerned with expanding an already expanded consumer market. And it has become now a dominating factor in American literature. If you can take this into consideration, we will go back to what I said about awareness.

Out of changes in the melting pot of America we had the beginnings of an American literature, one that reflected and came to terms with, in various ways, the nature of experience in America. It developed and used—used as a serious language of literature and often as a poetic language of literature—the common speech of Americans, and that includes Walt Whitman and Mark Twain. It includes books that, in the main, have only recently been discovered, like *Miss Ravenel's Conversion,* and it includes writers such as Stephen Crane and Theodore Dreiser. It includes the literature of the 1920's. It includes books like *An American Tragedy.* Today, most of that literature, if it is reproduced in the newer media, is deformed, and today an audience is being conditioned differently. An audience is not being conditioned so much by education and by literature. When I was young we read to gain a sense of liberation, to gain a sense of expanded experience. Today television is giving a new generation the illusion that it is getting experience; but viewers of television are getting the surfaces of experience and little more. In addition, popular songs, which for the most part are becoming cheezier, are a substitute for poetry. So that the functions of contributing toward awareness and of intensifying understanding, which American literature *was* performing and was performing, on the whole, in a healthy way—*these* have been seriously disturbed by the new communications industries, not because they are new and not necessarily because they are directed toward a mass audience, but because they are directed toward a mass audience under certain conditions. In the case of television, the conditions are that it must sell goods and that everything else is secondary; and the treatment of human experience is secondary to the selling of goods. And in the case of motion pictures, they must gross so much, they must make so much money, that they have to deal in the most standardized common denominators and clichés.

There has been a change in the reactions and the feeling of the audience toward books. And—I hope I am wrong here, but I sense this change in many younger people. I know, for instance, in New York City, a year ago, I initiated a series of educational lectures for the Liberal Party of New York State, for the benefit of young liberals connected with that party. The Liberal Party of New York State is like the Democratic Party, except that it is a separate party and it often fights Tammany Hall and so on. And I found that twenty-five percent or so of my audience of, say, two hundred were against me on the question of censorship. They thought there should be a good deal of censorship. One boy got up and said that certain kinds of books make him have sinful thoughts—make him feel bad, make him feel evil—and so they should be suppressed. It never occurred to him that he might exert some self-control. And, on the whole, there is less reading. In literature courses today, students will read the books assigned to them and nothing more. When I was in college, we didn't study Theodore Dreiser, we discovered him; we went and got his books and read him. We discovered Sinclair Lewis, we discovered *Ulysses,* and we did so because there was a feeling that from reading came some sense of inner liberation, some more important and significant contact with life; you could expand the boundaries of your own sensibility and your own awareness. There was a growing audience for literature, and today the audience is largely declining.

At the same time that the audience is declining, we have certain new tendencies in criticism and in literature itself. Henry James was a great, or if not great, an extraordinarily skillful and dexterous writer; he was an honest writer. Some of his writing, particularly his more simple writing, like *Daisy Miller* and *Washington Square,* is lovely. The portrait of the young girl in *Daisy Miller* is wonderful for its freshness. But Henry James has now become sort of a promising young writer. We have what almost amounts to a cult of critics who believe in the doctrine of the total immersion in Henry James. The critic Philip Rahv, in a book of 243 pages, has 46 references to or quotations from Henry James. If Americanism and the American scene is discussed, Henry James must be quoted. Well, I don't care, and most people don't care, that Henry James became a subject of His Majesty, the King. He did, and that's all right, and who cares? But somehow it has to be explained if he's the prophet and the greatest critic of the American scene. And, of course, he wrote about a world that is past and dead in many ways; and he wrote only about certain phases of American writing. He wrote of it in relationship to awareness and in relationship to Europe. There were a few writers at the beginning of American realism, prior to Dreiser, who wrote about America this way. Take three of them. Take James, Harold Frederick—a book like *The Damnation of Theron*

Ware—and Stephen Crane. They viewed America in terms of European culture, and the difference between them and Dreiser is that Dreiser was trying to see America on its own terms. This is not a patriotic statement; it is a statement about orientation. It is a statement that intends to suggest that Henry James was not the be-all and the end-all of American literature, as the newer snobs make him. They have a notion that there is only one kind of book on one kind of theme that can be written, and that kind of theme is allegory; it is myth. For instance, there are so many interpretations of the myth of the whale that you become dizzy writing it. The critic Harry Levin, in a series of lectures he delivered in Virginia, pointed out that when Archibald MacLeish went to teach at Harvard, he attempted to find out what writers the students in his classes were interested in, and found that Hemingway was one. But every time the students wrote about Hemingway, it was as though they were searching for the Holy Grail— they had read a story about fishing, but it wasn't about a boy going fishing, it was a set of clues in a search for some profound symbol; and each one of them had to find a variation of the symbol, because if there hadn't been a variation of the symbol, they wouldn't have discovered anything. It's very sad. Think of it—these students, ten or twenty of them among the ten thousand people who have written essays on Hemingway and Henry James and Melville, and each has to find some point of originality; and they choose to do so by plucking out a symbol. They have a snobbish notion that they are the guardians of literature. They feel that there must be a symbolic interpretation of each piece of it that is different from the one that anybody else would make, and that all of it centers in Henry James. There are about five or six writers whom they write about over and over again. What's going to happen is that in five or ten years everybody will be so bored with the musings of these mediocrities that they will stop reading some important writers, James, Hawthorne and Melville among them.

There's another critical attitude at large, and it was revealed in a recent article by Robert Gorham Davis. He's an honest man, a teacher; twenty-five years ago, under another name, he thought that Marxism was the key to the universe. He was as silly then as he is now on the subject of the American tradition. He insists that a certain group of intellectuals can *will* a tradition, and that they have the right to will one. A group of newer critics, who have a talent for exegesis and skill in discovering ambiguity, have the right to imagine the meaning of the American tradition based on six or eight novelists as they are understood by them. And so from Natty Bumpo to James, with a little bit of concern for Dreiser—I mean for Ernest Hemingway and William

Faulkner—and on to Robert Penn Warren, who is greater than Dreiser and almost greater than Dostoyevski and Tolstoy and Proust—*that* is to be the willed recreation of American tradition and to be American tradition itself and if you don't like it, you are out of luck, whether you are right or you aren't.

This is a tendency that we have considered to be the advance guard. It is the advance guard in the sense that the baggage wagon of a train is in the advance; but it is totally irrelevant to the problems of coming to terms with American writing and irrelevant to an understanding of these new tendencies of our time that are uncontrolled and corrupting. We have a new world in which we understand very little, in which there is a considerable amount of disorientation, in which we are far away from a time, such as that of pre-Revolutinary France, when human and class relationships and human emotions seemed fixed. The world of the spirit of men is more uncharted than ever, and that being the case, the world of literature and art is more uncharted. At a time like this we have these two tendencies: 1) a tendency toward believing that everything is secondary to business and to sales and that, therefore, the purpose of literature is to produce a picture of togetherness like an advertising picture and, 2) the tendency toward snobbish so-called reinterpretation of American writing which is *not* a reinterpretation but is a willful sort of expropriation—an invention of symbols and attitudes that are pasted on to writing and then used to make a model for writing of all kinds. In a healthy culture, one tendency need not triumph. Many writers are irrelevant to everything that James stands for, and they are good or least there is a reason to think that they are worthy of consideration. Sinclair Lewis and Dreiser and a number of others. There are as many tendencies in literature as there are possibilities of sincere and honest imagination and expression on the part of those who contribute to it.

Well, now, all of this relates to the question of the writer and his audience in this sense—that there are larger forces at play in society that condition what can be—or rather what is likely to be—read, what will be accepted at one time or another. And these things have an effect upon what we will call awareness. Because one of the fundamental things that writing does is that it does, or *can,* contribute to awareness. Now I have attempted to give some perspective here, to give some frame.

Reflections on Time and Death

"Yes, the sun would soon fall behind the buildings on Wabash Avenue. Time. You must remember its awful meaning, even in the brightest moments of your youth. Time and Death, these were the enemies of man. There seemed to be a meaning hidden in the setting sun. That meaning was what? Death. And Death was a function of Time."

My Days of Anger

Q.: Do you think that Theodore Dreiser's novels should be taught rather than merely mentioned in senior high school? I am interested in what we are going to teach senior-high-school students.

A.: Well, I don't think it hurts them to let them read it. I don't see why it would. I don't believe in protecting senior-high-school students. I think that we are protecting our youth too much. I know there was a case involving my books and some other books in Philadelphia, and the judge said he'd rather let his daughter read these books than go in a barnyard. Now, I don't know, maybe he was right, but I don't see anything wrong with reading Theodore Dreiser. Of course, you see, in France there are a few things that are better than in America. A seventeen-year-old student in France, an ordinarily good student there, is superior to most of our college graduates. He will have read Zola and Balzac, and I don't know that he is any worse for that; I don't think books are so corrupting anyway. I think that is a lot of nonsense. Now, I would say this, that certain kinds of books should be read later, because they are overstimulating; but I wouldn't put Dreiser in that category. I would say that I wouldn't teach Proust in high school, or Joyce. The point is that I don't think you can *teach* books, but I would recommend them to be read and discussed. I don't know what's wrong with Dreiser's books being read in high school at all.

Q.: You might have a hard time convincing people about that. A situation I was in raised the question whether or not an eleventh-grade girl should read *Sister Carrie*.

A.: She probably would have thought *Sister Carrie* was old fashioned.

Q.: Can we do something to interest them?

A.: Well, you know I've sort of come to the conclusion that we should stop interesting them. If I were teaching, I would tell them, "If you don't want to be taught, get the hell out of here." I mean I've stopped trying to interest them. I really think we do too much. I think we're—you know, the policeman isn't the policeman anymore. He's a *pal* to little Johnny. The teacher is a pal, the old man is a pal and a dishwasher. Everybody is Johnny's pal, and little Johnny is just becoming murderous with pals. I just think there is too damn much effort to interest kids. You know, Bertrand Russell, in a book of his—and it's a very good book despite the title, *The Conquest of Happiness*—says, Why shouldn't children be bored? If they're bored, they'll use their imaginations, they'll have fantasies. And I think that what we're trying to do is to create a race of not quite idiotic, not quite intelligent, not quite civilized people, a curious race of some strange sort of animal that's always got to be entertained and to be happy, and can never be alone. I think that we should stand four-square for unhappiness for a while. Happiness has gotten to be awful in this country, and it's permeating the schools. I know. I've got a relative and I love him and I love his three daughters, they're relatives of mine, too, but I go to see him for two hours and I've got to play "piggy." Have you ever played piggy? You deal four cards to each person and an extra card, and you pass them back and forth and the first person to get four cards of a kind quits their playing. The last person who does this is a sixth of a pig, and when it's all done, finally, somebody is piggy. Well, I had to spend two hours playing piggy to keep them happy, so I don't go there anymore. You know, when I was a kid nobody did anything to us. They told us to get the hell out of the house and out of their way and it was better, we had more fun.

Q.: Was William De Forest a veteran?

A.: I think he was, yes. William Dean Howells praised his book, and yes, he was a vet.

Q.: We always refer to Stephen Crane as being the first American naturalist and the first man to ever write . . . a battle. Evidently De Forest preceded him.

A.: Oh, he definitely did.

Q.: What were your impressions of Crane's imaginative attempts at that?

A.: Well, I admire Crane a great deal. But I would not just think of the book as a war book. I think it's a book of growth. It's the story of how a boy becomes a man, too. And as Crane wrote, he wrote quite lushly and quite vividly. I think it is a very fine book, and it is extraordinary in that he never saw battle, isn't it?

Q.: Do you think his lack of experience created this lushness?

A.: No, no, because in his other writing he was the same. And then he wrote *Maggie, a Girl of the Streets*, and he wrote differently. He responded to life that way. I mean, the words denoting color are very pronounced in most of his writing. He apparently was more sensitive to and more aware of color than most writers. I think he was extraordinarily gifted.

Q.: *[Inaudible.]*

A.: Well, I made the point—that is, you see, there is first-hand experience, psychologically, and that is a different thing. It is often what is important. In creating Hurstwood—well, there was a kind of first-hand experience that Dreiser had. Before he wrote the book, he was in a very bad way; he was melancholy and had suicidal fantasies, suicidal intentions, living in a rooming house in New York. You could say that psychologically, he lived through a great deal of Hurstwood's experience. First-hand experience merely as exactly the experience that is described, that is one thing, but first-hand psychological experience is more important. It is more important to understand something than merely to see it. And that depends entirely on the writer—some people can get a lot out of a little and some people can see something all their lives and they're still blind.

Q.: You are now living in New York, and that city obviously has a lot of adolescent activity. As I recall in *Studs*, there was a transition, or a certain set of spiritual values, or a certain insight, which finally came to him in the end. In other words, naturalism purely as cause and effect began to diminish. I'm asking—I'm not stating, of course—if you were to write *Studs Lonigan* again, or if you were to write a story again about an adolescent in a big city, would you show the same environmental determinism?

A.: Well, I differ. You see, there is a certain misunderstanding there. I thought this book up, and I thought up the idea that Studs would die when I wrote the first word, and it was *my* determinism to kill Studs. Nonetheless, I probably would write it differently. When I was lecturing downtown at the University of Chicago and a couple of people from the old neighborhood were present, I pointed this out—that the children or grandchildren—you see, some of them are grandparents now—of boys and girls who grew up in milieus like Studs' don't follow the same pattern of experience now. They go to college. I mean, very few, particularly very few of the girls, went to college then, and relatively very few of them smoked cigarettes and so on—that's minor, smoking cigarettes. But the pattern of experience is different for those of that same milieu. If you wanted to find conduct parallels and that, you'd have to go to a poorer group and to those who are socially disoriented or socially unsure.

Q.: Do you think that the urban environment was what caused the action?

A.: Well, we really don't know what causes, say, a deterioration of a person, a life. We know some of the things that cause it, some of the things that influence it, and I don't think there is one thing that causes Studs to die; there are a lot of things. I mean if you want to put it on one thing, I would put it this way, that Studs makes the wrong decisions always; he never makes good decisions that will enable him to develop. I would say that Studs couldn't carry the burden of his own future.

Q.: Do you then disown the label of naturalism?

A.: I think it is misapplied a lot. I mean when naturalism was attacked, I accepted the attack, but I really shouldn't have. You see, it depends on what you mean by naturalism. Now the only really worked-out philosophy of naturalism that I know of by a writer is Zola's, in *The Experimental Novel* of 1878. Zola stated that there are two forces, heredity and environment, and that human action was the consequence of the interplay between them. He said that the novelist was a scientist and that his laboratory was life, and that there was no room or play for personal impressions—that that was lies and romanticism. Now I would—it isn't a question of disowning that. I don't think it is sound. I think it's an overstatement. He took the physiological ideas of Claude Bernard and just transposed them to literature. Well, I never thought that. When I was young there used to be much discussion of heredity versus environment and so on, and the only thing I could say is that there is an interplay in the same way that there is an interplay of man and his environment.

Q.: *[Inaudible].*

A.: Yes, in Thomas Hardy there was chance. In Dreiser there is the seeming play of chance. But Dreiser himself didn't believe in chance. Incidentally, Dreiser was not just a naturalist, he was a cloudy metaphysician; he believed in Christian Science, in yogism. Mencken said—I was talking with Mencken and he said, "You know, if Dreiser were ill and walking down that street and there was Dr. Ossler and Dr. Quack—Farrell, you could bet every cent you've got that every time he would go to see Dr. Quack." Dreiser believed in some overall spirit in the universe, he was very—he was a kind of a brooding mystic as well as an actualist, and he didn't believe that there was any such thing as individuality; he thought that we were all parts of some unknown cause which was a kind of brooding spirit. And Dreiser never thought things out; he didn't have a good philosophical mind and he wasn't very logical. What he did though—he grasped scenes, he grasped a situation quite fully. I don't think— quite frequently it doesn't matter what an author *thinks,* as long as he doesn't lie, because you find that so many different writers have different approaches, and it seems to me that this is only the sensible thing, because people are different and writing is individual expression. I think that there is just too much classifying; and there's been too much talk of naturalism without defining it, and then categorical renunciation. For instance, most contemporary writers are different from Dreiser in this way—they write from the standpoint of immediate experience. In that sense Kafka is much closer to people whom you would call naturalists than he is to Dreiser. Dreiser was more or less old fashioned, you might say. He used dialogue differently. He wrote from the standpoint of the omniscient novelist and his dialogue was usually illustrative. His determinism was often a fated determinism. He even went so far, in *The Titan* and *The Financier*, as to talk about Chemisms when Cowperwood can't stop falling in love or wanting to seduce every female he sees who is good looking. It was the Chemisms that were doing it. Well, I don't know. I got a letter from Dreiser once; he said that he had made independent experiments and had come to the same conclusions that Jacques Loeb had and it's all true. I don't know what it means, other than that it did seem to be meaningful to him. I'll tell you what *was* important and gave a sense of scope to his writing. It was the way he would ask the questions in a story that can be banal: What is the meaning of it all? He would dramatize that question in terms of a tormented or a, well, sometimes tormented life, full of clash and conflict, with success and failure, grandeur and misery, and so on. In that sense, his philosophical and mystical inclinations helped his writing, although they are not necessarily sound. Similarly I don't think that his moral point, his moral views—I don't think they're defensible.

Q.: *[Inaudible]*.

A.: Now John Dewey was a philosophical naturalist, but he wasn't amoral or immoral. It is relative, that is a different thing from saying amoral. Dewey was much concerned with ethics and Dewey's view was that the consequences are the test of an action, not the intention.

Q.: Do you think that in *Sister Carrie* and in *The American Tragedy* Dreiser took an amoral attitude toward the characters?

A.: Well, in a sense. I mean that Dreiser felt everybody was justified in terms of his or her own way of looking at things and that that was more or less conditioned. I would say that that was substantially the way he looked at things.

Q.: The attitude Dreiser took differed———

A.: Well, he was a little bit older and he had been working on that for years, and there was that side to him. He was a very brooding, sentimental man himself and I don't think—— When he was younger, you see, he liked to have a good time. He was fighting Puritanism, and so on, and he just, he made a different emphasis. But as he got older his mystical feelings really became uppermost; he thought of death and eternity. Of course I thought it was a good book, but a lot of people disagreed with me.

Q.: *[Inaudible].*

A.: In fact, I thought I would assimilate some of my own experience. But I don't know, it depends again on what we mean by naturalism. I would describe myself as a naturalist in the Deweyan sense, because I know of nothing supernatural that is acceptable to me. That is, anything that happens is subsumable by the natural, by what is called natural causes; and what happens happens in one world. In that sense I would call myself a naturalist. But that is different from what Zola says. I don't know, it may be that we are determined and it may be that we're not; I don't think it is a question you can prove. I think you can make as good an argument in defense of free will as in defense of determinism. It's not an empirical question; it's too big and complicated a question to be investigated empirically. It's a matter of opinion and logic, and in logic you can prove anything you want to, depending upon what premises you start with. For instance, in the Middle Ages, all of the proofs of the existence of God were based on the assumption that God exists. If you start out to prove free will by assuming that free will exists, you have proved it. If you start out to prove that it doesn't exist, you will prove that, too, and you will probably have been equally logical. But you cannot investigate the question empirically and come to a reasonably sound conclusion. I think that people waste a lot of time—I think it's healthy and natural to assume that we're free, that we have to be responsible for our actions. I think that's a necessary assumption. In education, if you don't make that assumption with children, you are going to have an awful time. You have to make that assumption in ordinary experience, and you have to make it in law. Society must be based on the assumption that the individual is responsible. And in education and psychiatry and so on, the individual must accept responsibility for his or her own destiny, and in that sense you assume that there is freedom, that there is freedom of choice.

Now, there are different kinds of force. If you want to return to the notion of forces at play, Zola thought of an enormous pressure or force of environment and an enormous force called heredity. Well, there is a certain amount of heredity, and of determinism in heredity. For instance, because either of heredity or of some kind of accident prior to birth, some children are born defective. Well, there's a kind of determinism there, or, if it isn't straight determinism, at least there is this much: There is delimited what can't be done. There are many things a defective child cannot do. You can find many instances in which there is determination or delimitation of experience. But at the same time, it's a fair assumption to make, and a necessary one, that there are many areas in which there is freedom of choice. And when we are in the midst of events—I think of this often in connection with history—when we're in the midst of events, we think that we have choices. When we examine a period, it seems as if certain things were inevitable. But even when it seems to us that events were inevitable and had to take a particular direction, at the same time, *we're* making a picture, we're making a coherent, sequential picture of events, and we're not taking everything into account. We're isolating. And we just happen to isolate in such a way that what happened seems inevitable. But I don't think inevitability and chance are provable, or disprovable.

Q.: In other words, accident is the whole optimistic world.

A.: I don't understand you.

Q.: Optimism is parents believing in the capability of their child to succeed in this country, to live and grow in a full life—God-fearing people, church-going people, sending their son out in an automobile and he's killed in an accident. We refer to it as an accident; we don't refer to it as any kind of divine plan. You can't accept the fact that this could be a divine plan.

A.: Well, I, you could accept it but I don't see the point. I don't see it's necessary to accept such a thing as a divine plan. It could also be that the child is predisposed toward accident, that he is a pathological driver and had that the accident was conditioned. Furthermore, I don't know why we should worry so much about happiness. Happiness is a by-product of living and growing. And you know, Nietzsche said that mankind does not desire happiness, only an Englishman does. I mean, we're crazy about happiness in this country. Most people are bored to death. Boredom is the new form of happiness, and so we're trying to convince the world that it should be the same.

You know, the notebooks of Samuel Butler—which are very interesting; I would recommend them to be read—begin with the question "Is life worth living?" And the answer is: That's a question for an amoeba, not for man. Despite what we say, we work on the assumption that we can make things work out well for us, that we have some freedom of choice, that we can attain some freedom. I would say further that freedom for man is a conquest, not a divine gift. Men have to earn and conquer their freedom. They become more free by gaining control over nature and over themselves.

Q.: Then don't we need what we have, or do we have a concept of accidents?

A.: Well, I would accept a concept of accidents.

Q.: There is more determinism in an accident than there is in parents wanting a child to have happiness.

A.: You see, if we're talking about science, then there is no such thing as accidents. Scientifically, anything that is an accident is a problem. You don't know the so-called causes of it. You see, we're talking of accident here in very big terms, and also in terms of the parents' attitude. The parents' belief is merely their belief, it has nothing to do with what happened—unless, of course, it happened to influence the conduct of the child in some way or the parents bought the car. But in the main, the parents are incidental in your whole situation. What we mean by "accident" is that something happens that we couldn't foresee, that happened despite what we expected to happen and what we did. That is, we choose a course of action and we expect certain results, we expect to attain something, and there is some interference of phenomenon that prevents it and we call this an accident. We get in an automobile and expect to go to a movie, and a drunk hits the car and kills us. We didn't expect this, so it is an accident. Now as far as what has happened at the exact moment in which the accident occurs—from that standpoint it isn't an accident. Given the fact that the car hit a bump or the man couldn't drive, it was inevitable at a certain moment that he would hit the other car.

"There is no truth without imagination."

Continuity and Change in Culture

Speech delivered to the sixth annual Piney Woods Writers'
Conference, Stephen P. Austin State College, Austin, Texas,
July 2, 1965

Dr. Ralph Steen, president of Stephen P. Austin College, made an introduction in which he noted that "At age sixty [Farrell] began a new series of books to be made up of twenty-seven novels. Age sixty is a time, you know, when many Americans begin to think of retiring, and when many others retire without admitting it."

Insofar as age is concerned, that is a chronological fact I had nothing to do with. I was not consulted about when to be born. And life begins again every morning. The last words of my new series of about twenty-five works will read (and the words have been used before— we rarely are original): "The world is forever old, and forever new and young."

I would like to make a second quotation. One of the great books of the nineteenth century is *My Life and Ideas*, the autobiography of the liberal Russian revolutionary Alexander Herzen. He was the father of all, or most, democratic ideas in Russia. Late in his life, when he was in exile in London, a Russian came to see him and said: "We educate one another until the day of our death."

Now, coming here isn't a bit of a displeasure or chore. It has been a pleasure, as I have met with a kind of friendliness that goes back to my own boyhood. In New York we don't have friendliness, you know; we don't have people. We have machines, and we have grasping hands pulling out our pockets in one way or another. So I stay in and write. It's easy to stay in and write. I have discovered that it's easy to stay in, and that it becomes progressively easier to write. All you have to do is keep your mind open. But it becomes progressively more difficult to be a writer. In 1945 I predicted this; I said that we were entering an era of bigness in literature and writing. The danger would come when outside Wall Street money came into the publishing business. And I also predicted that the writer would lose his influence and become a glamour figure. Once a writer becomes a glamour figure, he can be lied about every day in the week, and that's proper.

I believe in gallantry, but once I just about threw a woman out of my house. A group she represented wanted to start a new television program about handwriting. I said: "Is this going to be another Mike Wallace obscenity?" She said no. Then she came up to see me, and it was. They wanted to have somebody for me and somebody against me, and they were going to find in my handwriting personal traits that I felt were nobody's business. I told her I hadn't agreed to this. She said: "Anybody who's a celebrity has no right to privacy." I said: "You get the hell out of the house."

The reason I mention that incident is this. (I'm not going to go on to quote all the great intellectuals, but I am going to quote a third.) There was a great speech to the French Jacobin Convention by Robespierre called "The Principles of Political Morality," and in it was one phrase that is still pregnant to this date. It is "the dread of unimportance." We live today more than ever before in "the dread of unimportance."

Some years ago, a magazine asked me to go out to Milwaukee and write about baseball there. That was just at the time when the fans in Milwaukee had stopped cheering when the Braves hit a foul ball. You know—they actually used to cheer when a foul ball was hit.

Now, Milwaukee is a good town. It had one of the most intelligent mayors in America, Mayor Frank Zeissler. It's the only town I've ever been in, possibly barring the present one, in which the taxicab drivers praised the police. It's a town that the criminals try to avoid. I'm not going to preach virtue, but there's no dullness in certain virtues. There's no dullness in honesty rather than dishonesty, and there's no dullness in cooperative effort rather than built-up glamour—prefabricated, publicity-made glamour. We are on a dangerous course of producing a robot consumer, who when not working is supposed to spend his or her time looking at, and reading and knowing about, lies—or if not lies then inventions, foolish imaginings concerning those who are celebrated. In this system, the glamorous and celebrated and the unglamorous and uncelebrated are two separate classes of people. The first class is supposed to be living, and the second class is to live within the first, in the imaginative life of the first.

Now, I don't know what the hell "glamorous" is. I mean, I love life and talking of faith in the future—that's instinct. That's the grandeur, the nobility of men and women—that they fight and struggle for what they will never see, and that we live off the victories of our predecessors and pay them back for their suffering—those who have died and sacrificed their lives, and those who have suffered and those who have attempted to help mankind rise to its full stature. We gain from what they have done. It's more or less our duty to see that the future will gain from us in the same way.

In a political constitution, the living have rights. In any decent, moral and civilized society, the living, the dead and the unborn have rights. We have no right to contribute to the creation of a world in which the children coming into it will be turned into horrors. In passing, that's why I'm against Parent-Teachers' Associations. If I were a teacher and the Parent-Teachers' Association came to me, I'd throw them out, for the simple reason that it's enough to teach children for four, five, six, seven or eight hours a day—I don't know why you have to teach the parents.

When I was a boy, and I'm not harking back to the good old days, it was better to have your parents not interested too much. Of course, in those days, if you got hit and you went home, you never told, for then you'd get hit twice. But there were never real cruelties practiced upon us. We made our own play. We made our own games. Boys would even break up their own games. Well, in a sense, in art too we make our own dreams and fantasies; but not as a matter of making daydreams, whereby we quickly come to some extremely desired conclusion, such as the possession of Greta Garbo or a million dollars. We make our own fantasies and dreams in the sense that we conceive a world.

Literature and art are a world that man makes. I used as the title for one of my books the phrase "a world I never made," which I drew from the poetry of A.E. Housman: "I, a stranger and afraid, in a world I never made." In passing, let me say that I picked up a book on logic and language one day, and the author, whose name I would consign to my own forgetfulness, remarked: "That's a weak statement." And of course the character to whom it relates is a seven-year-old boy. But in art and in literature, we do make our own world. That doesn't mean that we have the liberty to make the world in any way we want. There's a sense of responsibility at work in art, as there should be a sense of responsibility in anyone, particularly anyone who has something to do with the destiny and the future of people, and with their souls. There's an appropriate phrase of Albert North Whitehead's, who was, I think, one of the great and stimulating modern thinkers, and who described certain methods of education as "soul murder." Words like that still have vitality, despite the publicity abuse of words.

In art and literature we preserve the memory of mankind; and without art and literature, we would live in an almost timeless present. We would have no measure of change. We would have no measure of valuation, except in our own immediate impressions. Concepts of science and history, the general ones, must be applied; continuity and change apply in literature.

Today there's a mood of almost total contemporaneousness among writers and critics, and when you have that you have a fear that the work might not be too good. That is what motivates many of my juniors, I am sorry to say, and I find that I am separated from them by a great wall, and it's a wall of mutual *dis*understanding. You see, I also don't believe in the methods of becoming a great writer that are used today. I wouldn't stab my wife, and so on. I would not engage in exhibitionism and justify it by referring to the fact that I am a writer. When you're *writing*, you're beyond good and evil. You're *above* it. You have to have sympathy and pity. It does not behoove you to play God or the Supreme Court. But as a human being, you have the responsibilities that others have, and you should accept them.

There's an old teacher of mine from the University of Chicago, Dr. Edwin A. Burke, who wrote a lasting book, *The Metaphysical Basis of Science*, which was one of the works written in reaction to nineteeth-century materialism. The Italian historian and philosopher Croce, in a book on liberty, said that practical men must look upon the poet, the historian, the philosopher as impractical men who do not know the world. Well, that's not true, Burke said. It's the poet, the philosopher and the historian who understand the world, and it is the practical man who manipulates it. There is as much fact in fiction as there is fiction in the world of fact, but there is a difference between manipulating the world and attempting to understand it. When we attempt to understand, each man's and each woman's vision of the world becomes important to us, because it is the most important thing there is to each of them, to each of us—ourselves.

In literature we stretch ourselves so that we are no longer just manipulating the world. I'm not condemning practical men here. But we live in very ponderous, momentous days. The twentieth century is the bloodiest of centuries, and the shattering of the twentieth century, which is the shattering of the past of mankind—that is, the traditional past, in the good sense as well as the bad—came with the First World War. All the ideologies, the ideals and the ideas that men held were ruptured, were shaken, were permanently wounded. In those four years of trench warfare, man's explanation of himself and his world somehow or other ended. By 1917, control of events was lost. Our whole modern society is based upon the conception that man can control events, that man can be the master of his destiny; that there is reason, and through reason, a world can be made that better fits the full capacities and potentialities of man. From that we have come to live in an ordered chaos. We have only fragments of traditions of all sorts.

133

Now to come back to fact and fiction. If each of us were to say: "What is the world to us?" or "What conception of the world do we have?" we would find that we have known and imagined things to be true. We have direct experience; we have facts drawn by inference, which is a legitimate process; and we have everything from truth to hearsay. Truth is concrete and relates to its situation, and with that idea we come to the interplay of continuity and change. The world is always changing, and yet there is a continuity. There are uniformities in change.

There was a woman who would have been a great writer, one of our greatest writers, had she lived but a few more years. She was a librarian in Atlanta, Georgia. She was born in Virginia. Her name was Frances Newman. She wrote two very good books with awful titles. H. L. Mencken and James Branch Cabell were much interested in her work, though they thought her titles were awful too. The books were *The Hardboiled Virgin* and *All Dead Lovers Are Faithful Lovers*. The books are not what they might seem. I have never read, particularly in American fiction, about the feelings and the sensibility of a bride as Frances Newman described them. This is not sensibility à la Norman Mailer, or anything like that. It's a *sensibility*. It's a feeling of fulfillment. It's a feeling of what a house means and what clothes mean and what a husband's friends mean—of what the change in life that is marriage amounts to. Newman was read in seven languages, and she was a very fine critic. She edited an anthology of short stories called *Mutations in the Short Story*. And she said that there was as much passion in the past as there is in the present, but that forms were more traditional. I'm paraphrasing her, not quoting her exactly. But techniques proliferate. They proliferate much faster than emotions do, and that is why, today, each story must determine its own pattern. She cited as an example Chekhov. I think that it's a good example. But it's not so much each story that must determine its own pattern as each life—I mean, each person must act to determine his own pattern of being.

One of our few distinguished, first-rate historians, Carl Becker, wrote a book called *Every Man His Own Historian*. Well, every person is his own literary critic. But to be a literary critic is not so important as to absorb something of what there is in literature, because literature gives a sense of added insight and meaning and dignity to life.

What is Art? It is a much misunderstood book. It is a book that has many good things and much of Tolstoy's dislike of experts. In it Tolstoy says that, thanks to art and culture, we can know everything that has been thought and felt in the past and everything that is being thought and felt today; and because we can, we are saved from being barbarians. Now, I'd say that we can't know everything. We can know something of what was thought and felt in the past and something of what is thought and felt in the present. If we do not know what is thought and felt, or if we do not know enough of what has been thought and felt, we still are more than lonely islands. I mean, we are somnambulists in a socialized world, because we live and think in each other. There are exaggerated and decayed notions of individuality current in this country. Man is inconceivable outside society. Man is inconceivable outside some relationship with other men. I say, "man"—that is a continuation of the domination of women. Should I say "men and women"? I don't want to introduce that question here, other than to agree with Bertrand Russell that men have the bigger muscles.

A concept that was important in the United States was expressed by the poet Walt Whitman, by the philosopher John Dewey. Dewey says that if there is any imperative, it is that of growth. Now we've had the notion that civil liberties means a right of dissent and that the right of dissent is the most vital aspect of freedom. Norman Thomas believed this. I say, dissent, yes—when there is reason; but the *value* and *need* of freedom is growth. And what is fundamental to growth is the culture of mankind. It's the continuity, the living continuity of culture. I am using "culture" in the narrow as well as the broad sense, because without the concentrated feeling and expression of experience in art, we are poor.

Now as I said, today the historic world is half shattered and half in change. We think of this condition as posing historical problems for us, and in the posing of historical problems our actual situation must be defined by an abstraction from it. Every posing of an historical problem is not a direct statement of reality; it is a generalization about what reality is thought to be. With that in mind, I want to read one quotation from Leo Tolstoy's *War and Peace*.

"It seems to me, because we see out of the past only the general historical interest of that period, that we do not see all of the personal human interests of the men of that time; and yet in reality the personal interests, the immediate present, are of so much greater importance that they prevent the public interests from ever being felt, from being noticed at all, indeed. The majority of the people of that particular period that was 1812 took no heed of the general progress of public affairs, were only enthused by their immediate personal interests, and yet these very people played the most vital part in the work of the time."

I want to relate that to what I said of glamour. The most useful people, or many of the most useful people, are the most uncelebrated. Many of the most useless people are the most celebrated. There was a time when I used to stand at my window in New York and look out and watch the garbagemen. I used to think: "Without them, we'd have an epidemic." They are much more important to all of us, they are much more important to me, than the fakers who are in publicity offices on Broadway and Madison Avenue and Fifth Avenue, who concoct stories. This is an age in which there is manipulation, and the human being is valued by his falseness. The false is treated as real and the real as false, and this is in the interests of a whole horde of columnists and producers; a whole horde of people who live off counterfeit art. The mind of this country is, unfortunately, too much controlled from the three centers of the communications industries in Washington, New York and Los Angeles.

I mentioned Milwaukee. The people of Milwaukee had lost their pride. They felt that other people were interested in Milwaukee only because it had a baseball team. Well, baseball is all right. I used to love it. I've written about it, and I used to like to play. I'm a sort of walking encyclopedia of the game up to a certain period, but baseball alone is not what makes a city, and public notice from others is secondary. Of course there is a kind of public notice that we value permanently, like humanizing yourself so that there's a light inside you, and that's true of a city, too. It is when the private and personal interest is more than just a process of fakery and grabbing, when it is comradeship, that public notice counts; and to Walt Whitman, democracy was comradeship.

The idea of democracy originally was growth, development. It doesn't matter how big or little a city is. But in America today we have a centralized, counterfeit, commercialized art, and it feeds nothing but our daydreams.

Years ago I read an article that influenced me profoundly. It was by George Herbert Mead, a colleague of John Dewey and one of the most suggestive and stimulating of American thinkers. Mead never wrote a book. His books are copies of his students' notes. He had a sense of change to such a degree that he didn't want to overcrystalize any thought. There's an article of his, though, in the *International Journal of Ethics*, on aesthetics. He treated aesthetics as serial processes leading to an end or a culmination. He made a distinction between the functional and the aesthetic. The functional was what you wanted in order to get on to the next step. It was doing one thing after another—using the means, and taking the necessary steps, to reach a desired end. But when you pause and contemplate the pleasure and the joy and the satisfaction you will get or gain at the end of this serial process, that is aesthetic experience.

Well, I would say that all experience is both aesthetic *and* functional—or should be. When we are working to achieve something, that is, when we are working towards an end, the joy of anticipation and achievement is great. But we can't work toward any one end alone except at the expense of other ends, and this is particularly true of the artist. It is not for him to work only for himself; rather it is for him to render multiple experience as best he can—to render it with the hope that he will leave some of it to the memory of mankind, because in the first, in the last and in every analysis the memory of mankind is what sustains us. In it is the source of all belief and of all faith. And I would say this: If you do not have something that is beyond yourself to live for, it's a pitiful and a mean little life you're living.

That's why, for instance, although Descartes was a great thinker, a great mathematician, his principle of doubt is not a good beginning for the process of knowledge. The best criticism of it was written by the American, rather erratic philosopher Charles Saunders Pierce, who said it is not doubt, but belief, which is the beginning of knowledge. And that is true in everything we do. Because if we don't believe that something can be done, we're not likely to do it. If we don't believe in the value and dignity and significance of men and women, we're not going to act as if they had any; and we are neither going to prove nor disprove dignity by logic. There are certain axioms of life, axioms that are the beginning of any process of effort, of any process of logic, of any process of knowledge. Now, in logic, these axioms are propositions. In other fields they are beliefs, matters of faith. In that sense, I have hope. I have faith. I think it would be unworthy of myself as a citizen of this country and as a person living in the twentieth century, and I think it would be unworthy of this country itself, to sacrifice its faith in order to become a comic Rome. Democracy was cradled in Athens. There was a period in Athens, an early period, when there was a grandeur of maturity in the history of man—the time of Pericles, which is so well described by Thucydides.

Thucydides seems to me as though he had lived yesterday. He seems very contemporary. He seems very contemporary because he catches the flow, the actual flow of people living, rather than twisting it into an invented pattern that gives excitement and action.

When talking about literature today, people often talk about action. Well, action can be of the mind. Action does not have to come to some denouement or some conclusion of a plot. It can be a psychological process. It can be some hurt or sudden joy. The value of a story can be simply that.

137

Particularly, we cannot put the lives of men and women, at a time when the pace of change is so great, into literary formula. Again, I would come back to Milwaukee. After I'd gone out to write the story, I wrote it; and I lost about fourteen hundred dollars that I couldn't afford to lose because the editor of *Holiday* Magazine didn't like it. He said I hadn't used fictional skills. In other words, I hadn't found Studs Lonigan in Milwaukee. You see, I killed Studs Lonigan in 1935. In the last volume, the nurse threw a sheet over the corpse of Studs, and then there were other things I wanted to do. I have always felt that a day in which there is not a feeling of growth, a feeling of some relationship, even if you're alone, a feeling of comradeship with your fellow men, in Whitman's sense—that is a day lost.

We all have the same mortality; and we all have some of the same basic emotions and needs. There is no ground to be snobbish. If we know more, we share it. If we have a special talent, it is our duty not to abuse it. A priest, a teacher, a minister, a scientist, an artist, a doctor—someone who has to do with the human soul, and with the fate and destiny of man—to me, such a person has no right to put his success in monetary terms ahead of the work he does. And so I would come back to the phrase of Alfred North Whitehead—"soul murder."

Now Alfred North Whitehead said that if modern man develops a new type in the West, it would happen in the American Middle West; and the consciousness of America as we know it—and as the world knows it—has come out of the Middle West, and, focused in Chicago, come into literature. In Texas there is a similar potential for cultural development, and although I'm not trying to flatter you, it is one of the few places in America where there *is* so great a potential. It would be a joke and a crime if it went unfulfilled. Texas is not South or North—it's Southwest, and it has a sense of its separate identity. You know more about it than I do—you're Texans; I'm not. But the few times I've been here, I've seen and felt the variety of the Panhandle and the Rio Grande Valley, of the Spanish background, the Mexican background. There is much, not of conflict, but of difference within the state, and there is a sort of energy here. And if Texas does not make a contribution toward restoration of American literature and culture that is free of the glamour merchants, that would seem to me to be a crime against the future. It would be failure to do one's duty, for men have a duty to think and feel honestly, and men have a duty to give to one another honestly their thoughts and feelings.

We must always remember, no matter how mechanized we get, Walt Whitman's phrase "the single solitary soul," and that the thoughts of that soul are part of the story of mankind. In the evolution of the generations, sorrow and suffering are redeemed and given meaning and dignity by what successive generations do and by the way they preserve the memory of it. Memory of it is both what is imagined and what is actual, because we do not have an absolute picture of truth. There is no truth without imagination. Knowledge is a creation of man.

Viedt has a phrase, "the innocence of the world," which describes the world before man works upon it. If man would manipulate the world only to "construct," that would be one thing; but when there is manipulation of others in order to create a career for yourself and in the process you create a phony sense of human beings, that's another.

Now, I stand on these principles and I have attempted to write this way. And although I'm sixty-one years old now, I intend to write until I gasp for my last breath; and one of the things that I don't like about death is that I won't be able to describe it. I think it is vulgar for man to be afraid, and I think the fear of death is vulgar, and I want no part of it.

The greatest crises men and women face are the last crises, and the nobility of man is shown in the end—by how he goes to Nirvanha, like Nehru. He died, as they say, with his boots on—he died in service. He died in service to his country, to his world; but there are various kinds of great men. The great man we truly admire is the great man who has a moral influence. Who lives beyond himself, lives for others—and not in a sentimental sense. I interviewed Pandit Nehru. The last time I saw him, in his palace in Delhi, I used the word "underdeveloped"; I said, "If you are underdeveloped, we are overdeveloped." He said, "It's humiliating to talk always of our underdevelopment." And it's humiliating always to talk about superiority and inferiority. Equality is not a question of whether everybody is equal in apportionment of brains. Equality is a matter of everybody being equal in the sense of justice, and means that everybody has a humanity that is part of the whole, that links us all together. That is the source of my hope, my faith and my belief. That is what will keep me going as a writer for a long time yet. If I should ever reach the point at which I have nothing to say, I will quit and do something else. With that, I'll say nothing more. If you say too much, you say nothing.

Danny O'Neill's Medieval Fantasy

The chimes had tolled "Nearer, My God, to Thee." Drowsy, he had imagined he was hearing the Angelus bells sing out from a medieval monastery. He'd visioned brown-robed, barefooted monks pausing from their labors in the field to kneel and pray to Mary. He'd lost his sense of time and place, and for a few moments he had believed, as in a dream, that he was actually watching, hearing the monks pray in the fields. Then the illusion had snapped. An intense longing had overcome him, a longing that had been almost unbearable. He had yearned to be living in the Middle Ages. The medieval centuries had risen in his mind, timeless, peaceful, sunny. He had thought of all those dead years rolling daily over the world while men had dedicated themselves to prayer, to the aim of achieving bliss in another world, to God.

My Days of Anger

"There is no more fixed meaning to a complicated work of literature than there is to a human personality."

Farrell on His Writing

Speech delivered at Miami University, Oxford, Ohio, March 14, 1957

I'm very glad that I could come back here. I feel a little bit shy talking about my own fiction. I have lectured so often that I have run out of subject matter, and I let Professor Branch more or less inveigle me into agreeing to speak about my writing. But I think that if I am very honest with you I probably will not serve my own interests, at least financially; because once I finish a book, I dislike or hate to read it. The only time that I will ever read a book of mine with real intensity is if I have to testify in its defense. I have looked through and thought about various books of mine, but the only one that I have ever read closely after I have written it is *Studs Lonigan,* and that was some years ago, when I had to testify in a censorship case in Philadelphia.

Young people agree with me about not reading my books. *Time* magazine once said that I was the worst writer in America, and for all I know they may be right. There is no absolute way of judging whether a book is good, or purely awful. The moment we try to establish absolute, universal standards for the judgment of books, we are liable to find ourselves becoming confused. The moment we try to establish laws or categories of determination, or some set of fixed criteria about what a book should be in order to be a good book, we will discover that we have examined books from the standpoint of the past—books that have been liked by persons by whom one is attempting to establish those criteria, or else books that are generally accepted as being lasting, or good, or great. But once we do that, we will find it as likely as not that a new generation will come along, or a new writer will arrive, and ignore all of our criteria—the writer will write in complete violation of the categories we establish. And if we happen to read him and like him he will violate either our standards or our enthusiasm. Try to imagine having set up some set of rules for what a novel should be prior to 1922 or therabouts, and then imagine yourself sitting down to read James Joyce's *Ulysses* and liking it—what would your rules have meant?

Quite frequently I'm asked questions about writing. When younger people ask me whether they should or should not become writers, I'm reminded of a story that the poet Carl Sandburg was said to have told on a television program. He told the story of Ty Cobb, the great base-ball player. He said that a sporting writer who had been following the Detroit Tigers for many years finally came up to Cobb one day in a ho-tel lobby. The sports writer said, "Ty, I've been watching you slide to second for ten years now," adding that he had discovered that there were ten ways Cobb slid going into second base. "And I was won-dering at what point when you are running between first and second do you decide which of those ten ways you are going to use." Cobb looked at him in bewilderment and said, "I jus' slide." Frequently, it's the same in writing—you just write. I recall that when I was a young writer, after my first books began to appear, I would read reviews of them and would discover that I had all sorts of purposes and was try-ing to do all sorts of things of which I had been totally unaware. And I thought about that, and I decided—I recognized—that if I confused myself by allowing myself to believe that I was trying to do what other people said I was trying to do, I wouldn't know whether I was coming or going. Sometimes I'm aware of purposes and motives of mine and sometimes I'm not. Sometimes, after I've finished something, I find that there's more involved in it than I'd realized.

My younger brother happens to be a psychoanalyst. He makes a good living out of it. I should say that it is a much better profession than being a writer. People come to him hour after hour, day after day; they lie down on a couch and relax, and he sits behind a desk, and they talk and he questions them, and they talk, and this goes on for one, two, three or sometimes four years, at fairly expensive prices; and they are trying to find out why they did something. All of us do not need to go to my brother, although it would be good for the family if all of you *did* go; but those of us who don't need to go don't know why we do everything we do. We don't fully know our motives. We are not fully aware of all of our intentions. This is true in normal living, and to some degree it is also true in writing. I have always believed that we write out of the unconscious, and that when we have what we call a clear path from the unconscious, we write better.

Now, this may or may not apply to all writers, and it applies dif-ferently from one writer to another. There are writers who are ex-tremely conscious and aware; they think that they are trying to achieve certain aims in certain ways, and they can measure what they have done and decide whether they have succeeded or failed. Henry James was a writer of this kind, and he was a writer of extraordinary skill; James Joyce was also a writer of this kind. But even among these, and even when a writer states his intentions—and any time a writer states his intentions or states an aesthetic, remember this: that a writer's statement of an aesthetic differs from a critic's or an aesthetician's; the writer may say that something he believes is universal for all writers and as likely as not it will not be true, but it is valuable and useful and important to him; whereas an aesthetician or a critic will state it with a different purpose, as his judgment of what constitutes aesthetics in terms of works he has read or of works he would *want* read. And similarly, when a writer states his intentions, it's often easy for him to rationalize.

Many of the formative writers and thinkers whom I've read, and who influenced me very much, were American pragmatists, among them John Dewey, the late George Herbert Mead and William James. I agree with William James that a person has many selves, and I more or less agree with the conception of character to be found in the writings of James and Dewey and Mead, a conception of character in which you concede that there is a functional relationship between character and environment. Now, when I was young and first beginning to read books, one of the big issues of the time was whether character is formed by environment or heredity. In passing, that is the basic theme in the work of Emile Zola, who believed that science had proved that heredity was the dominating influence, although both environment and heredity formed character. I never could accept that view. I felt that there were things we do not know completely about how character is formed—that character is a social product, a result of our having lived in society.

Now another influence on my thinking was that of Freud, but I think that there is a consistency between the criticism of Freud and the writings of Dewey and Mead and James. As a matter of fact, there is an extraordinarily interesting and original book—a book about which I would hazard the statement that it is a contribution to psychology and psychiatry—called *The Idea and Appearance of the Body Image,* written by a refugee psychiatrist who now is dead—Schilder. Schilder studied how we develop our own body image, and by "body image" he meant our total sense of ourselves, including our visceral sense of ourselves. He studied and dealt with the question in neurological and sociological-psychiatric terms, and he came to a conclusion that is completely consistent with the conclusion about the relationship of character or self to environment that is stated or implied in the social psychology of James, Mead and Dewey. When I began writing, some of these issues were more or less in my mind, and to the degree that I was conscious of intentions, I attempted to present character in those terms. Behind that theme was also a feeling, or a hope, or a desire, that I would present a character so that the reader felt the character was living, was acting out of his full life experience at every moment. In attempting this, I did not feel that I was illustrating any one specific thesis, or that I was dealing with philosophical problems, or even with sociological problems as sociology; I felt that this was the most important thing in fiction—the most important attainment of a writer—the making of characters who are alive. I believe that if you write a book and the reader does not feel that the characters in it are alive, does not beleive in one way or another that they are credible, then the book should be called a failure—it is wooden, it is dead.

Secondly, there are many different conceptions of time, and there are many different conceptions of space. When we think of the world either scientifically or in terms of common sense, we have one or another conception of time and space. But if we think of time and space in terms of our own body images—our feelings and our ways of seeing the world—then there are many systems of time and space. And in the same way there are many different meanings—of things, of objects. People look differently according to who they are. I more or less had these relative conceptions in my mind when I wrote *Studs Lonigan.* I don't mean that I was attempting to illustrate them; but they helped me to see character, and helped me to discover it, and helped me to invent or pull out of my memory certain types of scenes and certain aspects of character I wanted to get down.

Thirdly, all of my early work was written virtually without notes. I don't want to refute critics here or to bring up critics who have passed into the shades, but although it was always said that I wrote with a notebook, the fact is that I wrote most of my books without any notes and that most of my books were based, in one way or another, on childhood impressions and memories. This doesn't mean that I experienced events or scenes or characters precisely as they were or as they happened. As a matter of fact, I have always preferred, rather than to have recourse to notes or documents, to invent. In passing, for instance, in two novels of mine, *Yet Other Waters* and *The Road Between,* there are a number of speeches in the case of which I preferred, rather than to read the speeches of the character who gives them, just to sit down and write them myself. But the material was the material of impressions of the years before I read much.

When I began to write *Studs Lonigan* in 1920, there was a wealth of undigested experiences for me to work with. Now everybody has such undigested experiences from childhood, and I mentioned somewhat flippantly that my brother is paid for listening to people find out why they did certain things. Well, what comes out is that they are trying to gain insight by plowing through their childhoods. On the other

145

hand, I had some conscious ideas about character and environment. Furthermore, all of us, to a larger or smaller degree, are children of the Enlightenment—I mean of the great Enlightenment of the eighteenth century. In the 1920's, when I was, to a considerable extent, intellectually formed, there was a kind of American Enlightenment and, as a matter of fact, one of its leading propagandists—in a sense, a kind of peculiar journalistic Voltaire of that period—was H. L. Mencken. He himself identified with the eighteenth century and looked back to it as his favorite century. There are two ideas associated with the Enlightenment that I want to stress here. One is the emphasis on reason and the rule of reason; the second is the sense of the dignity of the individual. Now there was a kind of unstated assumption in my books, in my attitude toward these two premises of the Enlightenment—one, that of reason; two, that of the dignity of the human being. And, the sense of some of the writing as I then regarded it was: This is not reasonable; this is not the kind of conduct, this is not the kind of society, this is not living according to the kind of values and these are not the kind of values themselves, which permit the individual to attain his dignity. . . . Those ideas were in my mind.

In the 1920's, and in the 1930's, too, there was a certain vibrancy in the atmosphere that there is not at the present time. I was asked just before I came in here if I thought that there were not similarities between the 1920's and the present period, and I said that I felt that there were more differences than similarities. The 1920's, as you have probably read and heard, were a period of personal and social revolt, and those who became writers—along with certain groups of students in the colleges—were quite militant. They were militant in the personal sense; they believed that this was the way to find individual freedom.

In passing, I would say that there is quite a difference between attitudes toward Freud in, say, the 1920's—the first post-war years—and the 1930's. In the 20's, perhaps, there was more insight about the significance of Freud, and more critical regard for him. But in the 30's—and I'm not talking about psychiatrists but about literary men, critics and others, who referred to Freud—in that period, Freud told you something about yourself, told you that you might have an inferiority complex and that you wanted to be free of it as quickly as you could. In the 40's, Freud was a means of getting into your past and explaining why you *couldn't* be so free.

Now, the major difference between the present and the 1920's is that the 1920's was in many ways a safe decade. It was possible for youth to revolt, to be antisocial, and not to be afraid, as youth and as everyone else is afraid today. There was great disillusionment about

World War One; but no one believed, and no one could conceive, that the United States was in danger, in any sense of the word. No one conceived that the future of the world could be in danger—the idea of the end of the world was theoretical. There were some of us who believed it in the sense that we accepted the second law of thermodynamics, which holds that there will be a leveling off of energy—there will be the predomination of a condition called entropy, where the universe is in such a state that life is not possible. Now, this was a purely scientific and theoretical conception and was conceived as the eventual fate of the universe, aeons ahead. That attitude is expressed in an essay that moved me very much in the 20's, and which had great influence, and that's "A Free Man's Worship," by Bertrand Russel, in *Essays on Mysticism and Logic.*

Today, that feeling of militancy does not exist—it does not exist even among youth. I'm not saying that it should exist. There were different conditions in the 1920's. We grew up at an earlier time, and with that, we conceived the idea that the writer must fight. Now, in a certain sense, this was called for then more than it is called for today. There was a different generation of college professors, and the modern American writer was still fighting for recognition in the academy. If any of you have read, or if you do read, the essays of H. L. Mencken, you will find that he is lambasting the English professors again and again and again. He lambastes them almost as often as he does the politicians, the Methodists, the wowsers and others. At one time, English departments were very prissy. Not only did they not accept contemporary writers; some of them, and some professors, including very distinguished scholars, wrote about the contemporary scene with a meanness of spirit. A very distinguished professor at Harvard, the late Dr. Irving Babbitt, wrote a book that I would recommend you read, called *Rousseau and Romanticism,* in which he practically destroyed every modern writer—every writer from Rousseau on—as a romanticist, and he used the most assiduous compilation of quotations in the history of American scholarship to do it.

There was a very distinguished professor at Princeton, one who has written some excellent essays, including an excellent essay on the poet Crabbe—the late Paul Elmer More. But when Paul Elmer More wrote about John Dos Passos or James Joyce, he showed a kind of meanness of spirit, and almost an ugliness.

There was a very distinguished professor at the University of Chicago—he was a very erudite man who made a record for himself in the history of American scholarship. We used to make fun of him; we used to say of him that there was more of Plato in his head than in any other two heads in the entire universe. It was the late Dr. Paul Shorey. If you dig back through the library files and read Paul Shorey on contemporary literature, you will find a meanness and nastiness of spirit in him, too. And the writers whose consciousness and whose intentions were formed in the 20's—these were formed against the background of what the academy was.

Today English departments are different, and as a matter of fact many of the teachers in them are products of that same revolt that Mencken promoted. Even in serious studies, Mencken continually, consistently spoke out against puritanism. Mencken's view of puritanism wasn't a complete and scholarly view; what he attacked as puritanism were these kinds of manifestations. By having done that, Mencken helped clear away a lot of ground, so that a member of a later generation—a young student in the 20's—was free to make more serious and worthwhile studies of puritanism, and this was Dr. Perry Miller of the Department of English at Harvard.

Now, the militancy was militancy against value—I mean, a rejection of many of the values of society. One of the books that had tremendous impact in the 20's was *Babbitt.* As a matter of fact, *Babbitt*—Sinclair Lewis, Theodore Dreiser and Mencken—were much stronger influences than Ernest Hemingway and F. Scott Fitzgerald, the writers who now are studied as symbols of the 20's. Hemingway and Fitzgerald were the young generation of the 20's, but these others were the men who were setting the attitudes of the coming generations. And there was that attitude that I have absorbed.

As a personal aside, I would say this—that the need to write is fundamental to the writer: his fundamental purpose, if we can reduce it to one purpose, is to find expression for himself. To express himself—that is important above everything else in the mind of the writer. And that need for expression is also revelatory of a need to live. Now, what I call a need to live is a need to live as a person of growing responses. Writing is a means of becoming more aware. It is a means of working out your own way of seeing and feeling life and giving expression to it. And, as such, it is a concentrated, long-term effort to do the same thing that everyone tries to do in one way or another. What a writer does is to take what is passing—what comes and goes as a kind of flicker in the minds of everyone—and to work it out. I mean, in the course of any day of any of us, we have memories, we have conscious and unconscious fantasies, we have daydreams, we have resentments, we have moments of elation, we have moments of despair; we look at various things and they excite us, they exhilarate us, they cause us to tingle or they cause us to feel revulsion. Well, the writer will work out such conscious experiences and embody them in something that he writes, and in doing so he is developing in detail what we more or less flounder through in the course of our own lives.

Now, I mentioned awareness. If we look at the history of American literature, we will find two things of importance here, one having to do with literary awareness, or tradition. America began with a low level of literary awareness. It was a pioneer country, many of whose citizens were the sons and daughters of the disinherited and the rejected of the world. It largely had a colonial culture, and there was, on the one hand, a different kind of awareness from the awareness that educated Europeans could have. On the other hand, there was little experience, little in the traditions of writing that could help the American writer to describe new experiences that he had. Now, the way I would suggest to make this point clear is to propose that you read a few early American works. I would propose among others that you take a poem called "The Day of Doom," by Michael Wigglesworth. It was published in the eighteenth century, and it is the *Inferno* of Calvinism by the Dante of the New World, of theocratic New England. It is a crude, awkward poem that justifies the Calvinist doctrine of predestination. At one point in the poem, Wigglesworth wonders "if unborn babies are predestined to hell, will they go there." For a moment he is troubled; but then he works it out. Predestination is right; unborn babies will go to hell if it is so predestined, but they'll have the softest place in hell.

But take any early American poem or creative work and compare it to the French writing of the time, and you will see a great difference. I will mention one of the first early great French novels—in my opinion, one of the greatest novels ever written, although it is not well known here. It is a book called *Les Liaisons Dangereuses*. It was written by a French military expert named Choderlos de Laclos. As a matter of fact, Laclos was an engineer in the French army, and he wanted to come to America to make his fame and make his name with Lafayette. One of the curious ironies of the history of American freedom is that, in order to have been a French officer and to have come to the United States with the Marquis de Lafayette to fight for freedom, you had to have a lot of money. Choderlos de Laclos did not have the money, and so he was disappointed. He wanted to be remembered by mankind, and he wrote this book. It's a story of what would be called a "wolf" today. In all events, it's the story of a seducer, and the book is presented in a series of letters from all the characters. The seducer, Valmont, is one of the most conscious characters in literature, and he plans his conquests as though they were an artillery campaign. What I

149

want to emphasize is the great level of awareness in the book—the characters know what they are doing, and the literary tradition is known to the point that the writer can present them this way.

In American writing there was not this kind of awareness; Dreiser and others who came before us didn't have it, and we ourselves did not have any clear-cut models to imitate from Europe. For us it was a question of writing, in part, to understand some of the features and aspects of the patterns of destiny and the types of characters of earlier American writers; and along with that, if we were going to develop, to come to terms with this kind of experience in the sense of emotional affirmation or emotional rejection, and in the sense of understanding it for what it was, and understanding it in terms of values.

Now, if you will mention Dreiser's work, I will mention the work of writers whom I may or may not like—Upton Sinclair's *The Jungle,* the characters of Sherwood Anderson, the characters of Ring Lardner, of F. Scott Fitzgerald, of Ernest Hemingway, of Thomas Wolfe, of Erskine Caldwell. They are all, as far as literature is concerned, new characters. They are all much different from the characters of European literature. This was a new material of life; and the language of American writing—the ordinary language—has been developed and perfected, more or less, to become a language of literature. New forms had to be created. It was necessary, also, to fight for recognition of this new material as a proper subject matter of literature. I was more or less aware of these things before I started writing, and, through the process of writing, I grew more aware of them.

Today, circumstances are different, but these things, in substance, are part of the background and represent some of the ideas I had when I began writing. I have not talked in any specific sense about my own books, or attempted to analyze them. Concerning them, I would say one thing. The meaning that a book has to a writer may be much different from the meaning a book has to a reader. The meanings will be different to readers of different generations. A friend of mine, a refugee scholar named Leo Lowenthal, once wrote a study of interpretations of Ibsen, and he found, in Germany, in a period of only thirty years or so, a succession of different interpretations—among the older generation of Marxists, the generation of Frederick Engels, for instance, and the younger generation of Marxist Socialists. When Nietzsche's work became popular, there was a Nietzschean interpretation of Ibsen. Each generation looks differently at books, and the meaning of books also shifts from reader to reader. There is no more fixed meaning to a complicated work of literature than there is to a human personality. But I would say, finally, that I have considered, have tried to explore the nature of experience—and to explore it frankly and directly. I usually and mostly have tried to write, particularly the novels, in such a way that when you're reading them you feel that there is not an author intervening—that there is only the unfoldment of the destiny of the characters, whom you can see, and believe are real, and in whose fate you are interested in one way or another.

Well, that is part of what I wanted to say here. I am going to stop now. I think it will, perhaps, be more interesting if we take some questions, if there are any you care to put to me.

Q: Do you have any certain time of day when you like to write, when it's easier to write?

A: I've got too much to do. I used to be able to plan to work in the morning, but now I work whenever I can. I mean, sometimes I do my work at night. I've come to like working at night better than in the morning. But I usually work all day—that is a matter of temperament. I had a friend who would write as a bird sang outside his window, and that may be a matter of idiosyncrasies. You have to discover how you can work best yourself, and what is good for one person is not good for another.

Q: You said that you are trying to achieve in your writing more or less a steady stream of consciousness, did you not?

A: No I didn't say that. I said that I attempted to write so that the reader doesn't feel there is an intervening author and senses the unfoldment of the destinies of real people. I have used what I suppose could be called a stream of consciousness in various books of mine, but there are writers who write in *steady* streams of consciousness—Sherwood Anderson, in *Many Marriages,* is one. Another American writer, who I think deserves more attention than he receives, both as a poet and as a fiction writer—Conrad Aiken—wrote a book many years ago called *Blue Voyage,* which did present one steady, internalized stream of consciousness.

Q: Do you get your inspirations from real situations? If not, from where do you get them?

A: I get inspirations from all over—sometimes from inspiration itself. I wrote a scene in *Studs Lonigan* with the boy, Studs, sitting in the park, and the girl, Lucy, in a tree. Well, the actual circumstances of that scene were that I always wanted to do that. Once I almost had a chance and I was too shy; so I put it into the book. Sometimes you write what you didn't do, sometimes you write what you did, sometimes—well, the point is that ideas are better than inspiration. You don't get inspira-

151

tion out of yourself; you get ideas—from anyplace, *including* yourself.

Q: What kinds of books do you suggest that a young author here at the university read in order to get a good background?

A: In part that's an individual matter for writers themselves. Just today I was thinking that we have a younger generation of critics, and many of them are teachers who tell young readers to read only the best, and only a few, writers. Don't read a number of other writers because they're dead, they're passe, they say. They recommend Tolstoy, who is a great writer, Henry James and a few others. But I think it is better to encourage catholicity. I know that as a young writer I read a number of books that excited me but that I wouldn't like now. As I was talking to Professor Branch today, I mentioned one of them to him, a book I used to like very much, called *Travels in Philadelphia* by Christopher Morley. Today, I think Morley smokes a pipe better than he writes—but I thought differently then. Theodore Dreiser was stimulated by Mary and Padraic Colum and by Eugene Field, who wrote *Little Boy Blue* and many other things. So I would encourage what will stimulate a young writer, what will intensify the taste for reality and the taste for experience.

Now, I would make some specific suggestions. I think that it would be very good to read the diaries of writers. I would particularly recommend the letters of Anton Chekhov and the diary of Stendhal. If any of you read Stendhal's diary, you will find there confirmation of what I say about considering your own experience; if you contrast Stendhal's diary with Donald Elder's biography of Ring Lardner, or with Dreiser's *Dawn,* you'll see the difference in how a writer's consciousness was formed in the United States and the Midwest and how it was formed in a highly civilized and cultivated country like France. And I would recommend the letters of Joseph Conrad and the letters of Marcel Proust. There is a biography of Flaubert put out by the Grove Press, and another of Chekhov, that I would also recommend.

The biographies and the letters of writers are among the things that I would strongly recommend. Now, as to their reading books of ideas— that depends on whether or not they are interested in ideas in the formal sense. Some people are and some people are not. In any case, the ideas a writer holds do not mean that he will or will not be a great writer. For instance, I think the greatest poet of the English language in our times was William Butler Yeats, and William Butler Yeats believed in astrology and spooks and fairies. According to report, a friend of Yeats, AE (George William Russell), who was one of the founders of the Irish Renaissance in the early years of this century and was a gifted poet in his own right, used to paint his visions and show the paintings to Yeats; and Yeats wouldn't believe that AE had seen what he painted, and when Yeats read his poems aloud AE wouldn't believe that Yeats had had the visions in the poems. AE was a fine poet and Yeats was a great poet, but I think that neither of them had ideas I would give a nickel for.

I have always emphasized that the more you read, the better. The more curiosity, the more taste for life, the more thirst for reality you have the better it is.

Q: Once you have written a particular segment of a book, how do you get away from it and look at it objectively? Most writers complain of being too close to the subject to look at it in relation to a whole.

A: Well, I'll tell you—usually I can't do that. When I finish a chapter, I start a new one, and I don't look at single chapters until I've quite finished the whole work. Sometimes I can't finish a story or some other piece of writing for a long time. I put it aside and do something else and pick it up years later. You *do* get too close to your material, and there is no rule about it; I mean, you get too close to yourself, too. That's part of the struggle of writing—trying to gain increased control, increased objectivity and a growing sense of what you are trying to do. Every writer has blockages, and every writer has moments when his confidence is low—what I do now is to keep myself at work on many projects, so that I do not waste time stewing about them. And when I'm blocked I just sit down with a notebook and practice free association. Another thing to take into account is that writers need editors. It is very hard to find a person who is a good editor, but if you've got someone you can trust and can bring your work to—well, maybe he might be the person.

Q: You were talking about the major influences that get into a writer, influences which have conditioned the writing of the experience. But the world is constantly changing, so how do you search for the new characters that you talked about?

A: For one thing, we don't have to search; characters are all around in America, and they *still* are. It is very interesting that you can find in American writing much more easily than in some European writing how the writers—how it grows out of their childhood. In Theodore Dreiser, this is much more so than people realize. You're not necessarily searching for characters. I think that when you go around searching for characters, you won't find them. What you're doing, is this— you're trying to get a better hold on the means of expressing your experience, or how you imagined your experience. You can say this about writing—that it deals with what happened, what might happen or what is imagined can happen. That is, it can be an imagination or a fantasy, or it can be something that has happened or ought to have happened—as, for instance, I ought to have sat in a tree with a girl—but you don't search, what you do is, you just try to become more conscious of yourself and others, and of the qualities and characters in life. That is the best I can say in answer. I hope that it is satisfactory.

George Raymond vs. Eddie Ryan on "As If" Philosophy

"You should read Vaihinger's *The Philosophy of 'As If.'* The world is really as if it were the world we think it is—it's inside our heads. What isn't inside our heads is only as if it were outside our heads and as if it happened to be the way we think it is. Time is one of man's *as ifs.* There's nothing right nor wrong nor anything else but thinking makes it so, just as our fellow superman, Billy Shakespeare, might have indicated to mankind."

"Everything in the world isn't as if it were what it is," Eddie said. "Rocks aren't as if they are rocks. They are rocks. They are something which feel hard if we touch them; they'll go through a window if we throw them." Eddie paused, groping for the right words. "What I mean is that, to us, the world is as we see it and think it to be, but the world is still a real thing. We can have illusions or false notions about it, but we still are in a world that is what it is."

Lonely For the Future

Early 20th Century
Trends in Realism

Speech delivered at Miami University in Oxford, Ohio, February
15, 1956, after an introduction by Professor Edgar Branch of the
English Department

*Ladies and gentlemen, a quarter-century ago, a story called
"Studs" was published in a magazine known as* This Quarter, *and
so Studs Lonigan was introduced to America. We know many dramatic and tragic characters in American literature. Hester Prynne,
on the scaffold in Boston, Captain Ahab sprewing forth hatred and
defiance by the mast of his ship, Jim on Huck Finn's raft, the once
brilliant Hurstwood, a broken man in a rented metropolitan room,
and Lieutenant Frederick Henry, hiding under a canvas, surrounded by guns and thinking of Catherine Barkley. But few characters in American literature arouse more pity for what might have
been and more terror of what is than Studs Lonigan, sprawled in
front of a fireplug at the corner of 58th and Prairie in Chicago. Our
guest tonight is Mr. James T. Farrell, creator of Studs, Danny O'Neill
and other memorable characters.*

*Mr. Farrell is a sturdy champion of realism in literature and free-
dom in society. His writings show a profound appreciation of ordinary people, a love of individualism, and an implicit idealism—all
of which appeal to his many readers.*

The word "realism" and the word "naturalism" are bandied about
a great deal. There are fashions in criticism, and there are fashions in
the way books are looked at. From generation to generation, it is
quite frequent that the same writer may be liked, and he may be liked
for different reasons.

Some thirty years ago, the school of American writers represented
by Theodore Dreiser, Sherwood Anderson and Sinclair Lewis, for
example, and championed by the late H.L. Mencken, were on the
march. They were giving shape to American writing. Today there has
been a strong reaction against them. This reaction is often presented
in the form of the statement that they were writing about what is
merely superficial—writing about problems and feelings that do not

concern us today; and that they did not create what some newer schools of critics insist is the only purpose of writing, some kind of myth, a set of allegories.

There have been many additional critical battles, in the past and in the present, concerning what is called "realism" in literature. In the book you use, *The Heritage of American Literature,* I was noticing a selection from a book by the late Irving Babbitt, in which he attacked Dreiser and Anderson and Mencken and Sinclair Lewis and John Dos Passos, and in which he stated, among other things, that they confound the difference between the real and the "welter of the actual." What Babbitt was doing there was presenting a dualistic point of view in which "the real" is more or less a Platonic essence—or to put it another way, the real is an idea and the actual, or the material facts around it, is not real.

Quite frequently, when writers are criticized or when theories or pseudo-theories about writing are presented and applied to them, the result is to confuse. So rather than attempt a definition of realism, I'm going to talk about some writers.

Sherwood Anderson was born near here, in Camden, Ohio, and as I was driven to Oxford today, I thought of him and of the time when I first read his work, in the 1920's. I thought particularly of four of his books—*Tar, A Midwest Childhood, A Story Teller's Story, Winesburg, Ohio* and a book that was published after his death, called *Memoirs.*

Tar, A Midwest Childhood is a kind of recreated autobiography of Sherwood Anderson's own life as a boy in a small town in Ohio in the 1890's. It is not strictly autobiographical; it is written like a novel. You know, Anderson frequently said that the writer lies. He didn't mean "lie" in the sense of mendacity; he meant that the writer imagines. *Tar* is Anderson's reimagined childhood. It's the dreams he felt and imagined, and it's the feelings he imagined he had had when he was a man in his forties and looked back on his childhood.

Now, all during the twentieth century, particularly in America, we have had what we will call a very fast pace of change. There has been constant alteration. In passing, for example, as I was coming here on a train, I was reading a history of the American trade union movement, and I learned that back before the First World War there was an effort to put automobile workers under the control of blacksmiths. Blacksmiths are a dying profession. We've seen many professions die. We've had the phenomenon of dead towns—of ghost towns. The small towns of Ohio of Sherwood Anderson's childhood were much different from the small towns of Ohio today—that was the age before the automobile; it was the age of the railroad. It was a period of great expansion and great hope. Fortunes were being made; new industries were being founded. We were on the eve of an era when business and management would march forward to execute billion-dollar industries, and the old craftsmen were dying out—the old craftsmen were being superseded.

When I first read *Tar* I was working in a gas station and attending the University of Chicago, and already I was living in a different world. The neighborhood I grew up in in Chicago was like a small town, in the sense that it was a more or less cohesive community. But there was a difference. It was a difference made by technological changes, by such developments as the automobile, and with these changes patterns of living were being revolutionized. Even so, I was intensely excited and intensely stirred when I read *Tar*. The cause of my excitement was the sense that if the fantasies, dreams and feelings of a farm boy in an Ohio town in a world that had already begun to change—if what went on in his head as he wandered through fields and through woods—if these things were important, if they were material worthy of literature, if they were what a distinguished and perhaps a great American writer would use in a book, then perhaps my own feelings were important. Perhaps the feelings of those with whom I lived and those who were around me were important, too.

Now, I put it this way because one of the fights that took place in an earlier period of American writing related to the type of character a writer created, to the type of character he used, to the kind of language he used, to scene and to setting—to what the late Dr. Babbitt called the "welter of the actual." You see, realistic writing in America was largely a revolt. It was a revolt against puritanical attitudes and a kind of prissyness, and against a set of overly conventionalized images of the world, which we inherited from the Victorian era. It was a revolt against what was called "the genteel tradition." Briefly and roughly, the genteel tradition was the set of attitudes toward writing and culture that grew out of New England and that had, among other things, weakened until there was an overemphasis on sentiment, an overemphasis on decorum and an objection to the development of the resources of the native American language. That revolt was related to the fact that during the later part of the nineteenth century, following the Civil War, the Midwest began to become a new cultural center of gravity, and there was a type of man there, a type of woman who felt, who acted and who thought differently from educated New Englanders.

The second book of Sherwood Anderson's I mentioned was *A Story Teller's Story*. In that book there is a little passage in which

Anderson tells of how he was sitting before the Cathedral of Notre Dame at Chartres in France. This Cathedral is one of the most magnificent structures created in any age and a peak achievement of the Middle Ages and the thirteenth century. Anderson, in looking at it, was moved to feel that it was one of the great accomplishments of the human spirit. But then he thought that the men who had built it were dead, and that his own roots and his own life grew out of the Ohio in which he grew up.

I mentioned a third book of Anderson's, *Winesburg, Ohio.* In an earlier period of our national life, the humor of our popular writing was based upon a kind of contempt for anybody who was different from the conventional image of an Anglo-Saxon norm. In passing, it is interesting to note how the artist, or a man of artistic sensibilities, is treated in the work of another early American realist, Frank Norris, who wrote *The Pit* and *The Octopus.* The businessman goes out and makes a living—he's cornering the wheat market—whereas the artist, the architect, merely reads Browning to his wife and talks about how the home should be decorated. And in general there was the conception that the artist was a kind of weakling, a man who was not equipped to deal with the important matters of life, such as making a fortune in the wheat market, and so on. Now, Sherwood Anderson called *Winesburg, Ohio* "a book of grotesques." The first story in the book is called "Hands," and in describing the character in it, Wing Hiddlebaum, Sherwood Anderson remarks that if you would watch his hands—and I am paraphrasing here—you would see many of the beauties of ordinary people. In another story, dealing with a woman, Anderson says that before a woman of this kind can be understood, many sensitive people will have to reflect a great deal and many books will have to be written. There is another story of a very inarticulate farm boy who feels that he does not belong to the community and who wants to be like other people. This farm boy feels that he should tell George Willard—a local newspaper reporter who runs throughout the stories and who represents something of Anderson himself—that he *is* normal, that he's like other people. He thinks about it and he plans to do it and finally when he comes to do it, he is so disturbed and so shy that he can't speak; so he takes a punch at Willard. I describe the story for this reason: It is Sherwood Anderson's pattern in all these stories to show a kind of lost creativeness, and the thing that makes his characters grotesque is that their lost creativeness, their thwarted love, cannot find expression; and so they become queer, they become odd, they become eccentric.

I mentioned that the prevailing idea of humor, particularly at that time, was to laugh at anything that didn't fit a norm. If you have studied earlier popular stories—the earlier stories of the colored man and of the stage Irishman—you've seen the characters in these stories are stereotypes of ineffective, humorous characters who are always genial but who cannot bear responsibility. In brief, they are made lovable by cliche but they have no humanity and no real tension in them. One of the great significances of *Winesburg, Ohio* is the fact that the story and the characters are set in definite contrast to this kind of pattern. They are beyond this sort of cliche and beyond conventional images of what people are like, particularly what socially or economically inferior people are like. In this way, Sherwood Anderson's *Winesburg, Ohio* ties up with the feeling to be found in Walt Whitman's *A Book About Myself,* in which Whitman celebrates American Democracy and American freedom, and, almost ecstatic, writes in a poem that was shocking for the time a little verse addressed to a common prostitute, in which he says, "Not till the world excludes you will I exclude you."

Now, in the latter part of the nineteenth century and the early years of the twentieth, there *was* an attitude of exclusion. One of the significant aspects of what we would call early American realistic writing is that it attempted to draw closer to the way life *is* rather than accepting prevailing conventional images of life.

I mentioned one final book of Sherwood Anderson's, his *Memoirs.* The reason I mentioned it was that the period of his childhood, the 1890's, was one of great change, and in his *Memoirs* he illustrates again and points out this pace of change.

A writer who came before Sherwood Anderson and influenced him, whom Sherwood Anderson admired more, perhaps, than any other American writer, was Theodore Dreiser. Theodore Dreiser's first novel was published in 1900. It was *Sister Carrie.* The book opens with a country girl, Carrie Meeber, on a train to the city. I spoke about change; American realistic writing came into being at a time when the town was triumphing over the country, and the city over the town. It is significant that in the opening chapter of *Sister Carrie,* we find a farm girl going to make her way in the city. When Dreiser was a young man his family moved from one medium-sized town in Indiana to another. The Dreisers could never really establish a stabilized life. The Dreiser girls were always getting into trouble. The father was more interested in seeing that his children were saved in the next world than that they were educated and developed in this. And then, at the age when Dreiser was what we now call a "teenager," he went to Chicago, which, at that time, was one of the most dynamic cities in America. The businessmen of Chicago believed that it was going to become the financial center of the world. There was a spectacle of grandeur and misery. New things were happening every day. There were the beginnings of great cultural development as well. This was just prior to the founding of the University of Chicago, which has since become one of the great universities of the world. And Dreiser, a boy in his teens, felt that Chicago was singing. And he thrilled to this singing, as he tells us in his book, *Newspaper Days.*

In all of Dreiser's early books there was a great deal of movement from city to city, and as the characters moved there was a sense of growing, of building, and at the same time a constant representation of this spectacle of grandeur and misery, of the weak and of the strong. Now, the essayists of what is called the "Golden Age" of New England—and there were great writers among them—did not have ideas that were adequate for an understanding of America becoming the greatest industrial power in the world. I mentioned before that there were many kinds of excitement in the late nineteenth century and that one was the Midwest becoming a center of gravity. Another was that American philosophy was born—particularly American pragmatism, the thought of Charles Saunders Pierce, William James, John Dewey and the late George Herbert Mead, which for many years dominated American philosophical thinking and which has been considered the unique contribution of American philosophy. There was a great development in science. There was the beginning of the attempted establishment of psychology on a scientific basis, and with that, an ever-increasing current of thought called social Darwinism, which was an effort to interpret economic development and other conditions in society in terms of the hypotheses and conclusions of Charles Darwin—particularly the idea of survival of the fittest. That was considered to be a sound and warranted scientific conclusion. And Dreiser fastened onto the ideas of social Darwinism.

At the same time, there was a changing attitude toward morals in the air. It was in that period that William Graham Sumner wrote his book *Folkways,* in which he contrasted moral customs, mores and attitudes in various kinds of societies; and the conclusion he came to amounted to a moral relativism. It was in that period that perhaps the most original of American social thinkers, Thorstein Veblen, wrote his profoundly stimulating books, among them *The Theory of the Leisure Class, The Theory of Business Enterprise, The Instinct of Workmanship.* In passing I might say that although Sherwood Anderson did not read Thorstein Veblen, it is interesting that his feeling of craftsmanship is quite like what Thorstein Veblen considered to be the instinct of workmanship. And while it is true that at the time there was a school of psychologists called Instinct Psychologists, who multiplied instincts, Thorstein Veblen's concept of instinct was much different. It was a concept that assumed, roughly, that there was a biological, an instinctive, a natural need to work and to create. Now, Dreiser himself didn't read many of these books, but he did read Herbert Spencer and some of the European writers of the time, and he absorbed these attitudes, as it were, out of the air and out of the social atmosphere.

Sister Carrie, to continue, is the story of how this girl, Carrie Meeber, comes to Chicago; she becomes the mistress of a salesman. A character, Hurstwood, whom Professor Branch mentioned, falls in love with her; he leaves his wife, they go to New York—he has stolen some money—and from that point on, he goes down; and it is a picture of the decay and the disintegration of a man. In reading it, one feels almost as if, inch by inch, he is slipping off an icy precipice. At the same time, Carrie Meeber comes up. She develops and becomes an actress, and, at the end, after Hurstwood has been a suicide in the Bowery, she is a famous actress and she sits rocking in her chair in a New York hotel, wondering and pondering what it is all about. Now, the fact that this was a story in which the wages of sin were not death caused considerable concern and worry in the house that was publishing the book. The publisher's wife read the book, and it was literally sabotaged. A few copies were sent out for review by Frank Norris, who was a reader and an editor in the house, but no one knows what happened to the rest of the books. There was the feeling, not only on the part of the publisher's wife and, in consequence, of the publisher, but on the part of other people who had a rather tight and rigid attitude, that a book like this was not only shocking but was detrimental to the social health of the nation. But fifty-five years have passed. *Sister Carrie* eventually was published and became recognized, not only here but also abroad, and Dreiser became a world-famous literary figure—he became a pioneer for twentieth-century writers, and the republic continues to stand. And, of all the books written in 1900, none is as much discussed; of all American novels, none is as much discussed as *Sister Carrie.* You'll probably read it in your courses. It's in a Modern Library edition, and no book is kept in a Modern Library edition unless it sells five hundred copies a year. It has sold that much or more for many years.

Each generation of writers who attempted to draw closer to what life seemed to be, who, in other words, ignored or attacked those conventional images of life, has met the same fate. At this point, in order to give you a sense of what attitudes were and how a more frank literature developed, I'm going to read a quotation that is fairly long. It's from the writings of the late H.L. Mencken:

> Here is one of the fundamental defects of American fiction, perhaps the one character that sets off sharply from all other known kinds of contemporary fiction. It habitually exhibits not a man of delicate organization in revolt against the inexplicable tragedy of existence, but a man of low sensibilities and elemental desires yielding himself gladly to his environment and so achieving what, under a third-rate civilization, passes for success. To get on, this is the aim; to weigh and reflect, to doubt and rebel—this is the thing to be avoided. I described the optimistic, the inspirational, the author's-league, the popular-magazine, the peculiarly American school. In character creation, its masterpiece is the advertising agent who, by devising some new and superimbecilic booby trap, puts his hook-and-eye factory on the map, ruins all other factories, marries the daughter of his boss, and so ends an eminent man. Obviously the drama underlying such fiction, what Mr. Rex Beach would call its John Henry plot, is false drama, Sunday School drama, puerile and disgusting drama. It is the sort of thing that awakens a response only in men who are essentially unimaginative, timid, and degraded. The man of reflective habits cannot conceivably take any passionate interest in the conflict it deals with. He doesn't want to marry the daughter of the owner of the hook-and-eye factory—he would probably burn down the factory itself if it ever came into his hands. What interests this man is the more poignant and significant conflict between a salient individual and the harsh and meaningless fiats of destiny, the unintelligible mandates and vagaries of God. His hero is not one who yields and wins, but one who resists and fails.

Now, I don't subscribe to all of that, but I do subscribe to part of it, and I quote it as an illustration. Mencken championed Dreiser, he championed Anderson, he championed Sinclair Lewis; he opposed the efforts of book censorship, and also, in 1918, he wrote the first edition of a remarkable and interesting book, *The American Language*. There Mencken argued that the language spoken and written in this country had become a language of its own—different from English—and that it deserved the right to be called the American rather than the English language. Now, whether we claim that that hypothesis is true or false, there is still a great deal of valuable, interesting and illuminating information in this volume, and in subsequent editions in which he added to it. Who in 1918 would have concerned himself about such questions as the influence of Chinese on the American language, the influence of Yiddish, the influence of the pioneer world, the influence of the Japanese? I ask that to emphasize the book *The American Language,* because ever since Mark Twain—or ever since the frontier humorist, whom we see most clearly in Mark Twain—there has been a development of more vernacular and looser and more flexible English prose. When Mark Twain first went East, by the way, there were objections to the way he wrote as well as to the fact that he made fun of the institution of royalty in a democratic country, and his books were banned from the public library of Brooklyn and caused some disturbance in Boston.

Mencken's *The American Language* emphasizes one point—that with the pace of change in America, there has been a constant change and evolution of our language. One of the features of American writing is the fact that a more common, a more ordinary, a more vigorous and more varied language has been used as an instrument of prose fiction, and, in Carl Sandburg, as an instrument of poetry, and this was also a break from the genteel tradition. One illustration of this, if you recall *The Adventures of Tom Sawyer,* is the parodies of the kind of language used in the stories and used in the fantasies of Tom. There was deliberate parodying on the part of Mark Twain, and it is in striking contrast to the language he used in his masterpiece, *The Adventures of Huckleberry Finn.*

Now, the remarks I have made have all been an attempt to make concrete one simple point, or two: first, that what was called earlier American realistic writing—I mean some of the writing that has shaped American literature of this century—in one way or another reveals an emphasis on coming to franker and clearer terms with the nature and the character of American life and, second, an emphasis on expressing it in a language that relates to the language of the people who live in American life and who are described. Frank Norris remarked in one of his essays that a literature that cannot be vulgarized is no literature at all, and will perish. What Norris meant was that this new and evolving and developing American language *was* a language of literature.

I've spoken of Dreiser, so I will refer to his book *An American Tragedy.* The reason I will refer to it is that it occurs in the 1920's, and I want to emphasize a change that has been reflected in American culture since then. I've alluded to the fact of change and pointed out that great industries were being developed, new occupations coming into being and old crafts being superseded. Now, by the end of the First World War, the United States had become a great world power and the chief producer of industrial goods in the world. There were many new war millionaires and a larger and more prosperous middle class—it was a prosperity that doesn't match our own prosperity, but it was considerable—and with that there came a greater emphasis on leisure. With the beginning of the success of the movement for the shorter work week, leisure and consumption—the consumer goods industries—gradually became more prominent. And in the 1920's, this is to be seen not only in entertainment but also in culture. Nowadays, generally speaking, culture and entertainment are linked. In the 1920's the Book of the Month Club was founded, new publishing houses were founded, new communications industries such as radio were developed, investments in the movies were expanded, talking pictures developed, etc. And the same way, entertainment—there was a wave of Chinese chop suey places where college students would go, popular dance halls with furniture imitating French palaces, etc. There was great development in advertising. In brief, consumption became a more significant factor in our experience. And in turn, the life of leisure and consumption began to become a more significant theme in our literature—in both our serious and our popular books. I quoted H.L. Mencken and one might say that Mencken's criticism of American life was, in essence, related to these developments; for instance, what Mencken criticized many Americans for was that they weren't civilized and didn't enjoy the civilized virtues—they didn't drink good beer and eat good foods and read good books and have good conversations and so on. In other words, they didn't know how to use their leisure. That is also one of the elements of *Main Street* and the revolt of Carol Kennicott.

Now, I would like to point out one aspect of *An American Tragedy* that relates to all this. The book is the story of the boy Clyde Griffith. Clyde's boyhood is what we might call socially eccentric. His father is an itinerant religious salvationist who preaches on street corners. Clyde isn't rooted in one place, and he doesn't feel that he belongs; he doesn't gain any sense of belonging. When he's fifteen or sixteen, he gets a job as a bellboy in a hotel in Kansas City and that is where he begins to acquire some sense of values. Dreiser alludes to something we might call a kind of American "hotel culture," in this section; in hotels there is a great deal of spending, a great deal of so-called looseness, and anonymity, and so on. Clyde Griffith absorbs his first sense of values from this; he does so after he's lived in such a way that no one has told him anything about how to live. The boys steal a car—he's involved in it—and he runs away and drifts from job to job. The jobs described in *An American Tragedy* very closely parallel the jobs that Dreiser himself had as a youth, and the experiences and feel-

165

ings of Clyde Griffith relate to Dreiser's own early years in Chicago. Clyde meets an uncle of his who owns a shirt factory in Lycurgus, New York. He is brought in to work in the factory, and he begins to conceive an ideal of success by connections. It is interesting that the description of rich girls—of the rich in general and the use of leisure—is different from what it was in Dreiser's early work such as *Jennie Gerhardt, The Titan* and *The Financier,* and *Sister Carrie.* In the earlier novels, when characters succeed on a material plane, they do it out of something in their own natures. But when Clyde Griffith uses his own capacities to succeed, he's frustrated. He has as much business ability as his cousin, but he's a poor relation. He can live neither with the workers nor with the rich set around his relatives, who own the factory that dominates the town. He remains socially abnormal and develops his idea of getting along in the world through connections; he becomes entranced with a conception of luxury first implanted in him as an inexperienced, bewildered and uneducated bellboy in a Kansas City hotel, where there had been—and now there is again—a continuation of the same kind of social eccentricity he had experienced as a boy—a social abnormality not rooted in an integrated life. In Lycurgus the distortion of his own sense of values ends in a tragedy in which he attempts to kill a girl. At the last moment he does not do it, but she drowns and he is captured. Now, until this point no attention, or not much, has been paid to Clyde Griffith. But all at once the entire force of society is put into operation to ferret out every fact of his life that can be found, and Clyde Griffith goes to his death in the electric chair.

The sense of there being an American tragedy in Clyde Griffith's story is that there has been a distortion of values. Clyde gives up and desires to kill a girl—Roberta Alden—who is warmhearted and who is capable of growth, in order to marry a rich girl who treats him as a mere object of vanity and social revenge. She has become interested in Clyde in order to flout his rich cousins. The tragedy is the tragedy involved in the distortion of social and moral and human values, if we may use those words.

Now, I would add one point. The significance of early American realism, including of *An American Tragedy,* has been its attempt to get more at, to explore, to reveal, to recreate the nature of experience in our time, in our society. In doing so, it has attempted to make characters more real, and by making them more real to give them a deeper humanity—the humanity of those who suffer, who are confused, who struggle, who grope and who may fail or succeed but who do so as it is done in real life. Along with that, realism deals with and is a comment on—and has been something of a revelation of—what kinds of costs have been paid for the pace of our change, for the expansion and development of this country. I think that this is part of the relationship of American realism to American life. I won't give you more examples, but I think that Dreiser, Anderson and Mencken serve as three significant ones. Today there are different tendencies at work in literature, but I would say that these writers have made a lasting and most significant contribution toward developing a clearer, franker and healthier outlook on characters and events, on human beings and on the nature of our common American experience.